GREAT
WRITING 1

Great Sentences for Great Paragraphs

FOURTH EDITION

KEITH S. FOLSE
UNIVERSITY OF CENTRAL FLORIDA

APRIL MUCHMORE-VOKOUN
HILLSBOROUGH COMMUNITY COLLEGE

ELENA VESTRI SOLOMON
KHALIFA UNIVERSITY OF SCIENCE, TECHNOLOGY,
AND RESEARCH, UAE

NATIONAL GEOGRAPHIC LEARNING | CENGAGE Learning

Australia • Canada • Mexico • Singapore • Spain • United Kingdom • United States

Great Writing 1: Great Sentences for Great Paragraphs
Keith S. Folse, April Muchmore-Vokoun, Elena Vestri Solomon

Publisher: Sherrise Roehr

Executive Editor: Laura Le Dréan

Development Editors: Yeny Kim, Charlotte Sturdy

Director of Global Marketing: Ian Martin

International Marketing Manager:
Caitlin Thomas

Director of Content and Media Production:
Michael Burggren

Senior Content Project Manager: Daisy Sosa

Senior Print Buyer: Mary Beth Hennebury

Cover Design: Christopher Roy and Michael Rosenquest

Cover Image: DAVID DOUBILET/ National Geographic Stock

Interior Design: Aysling Design

Composition: PreMediaGlobal, Inc.

U.S. Edition

ISBN-13: 978-1-285-19488-2

International Student Edition

ISBN-13: 978-1-285-75059-0

National Geographic Learning/Cengage Learning
20 Channel Center Street
Boston, MA 02210
USA

Cengage learning is a leading provider of customized learning solutions with office locations around the globe, including Singapore, the United Kingdom, Australia, Mexico, Brazil, and Japan. Locate our local office at: **International. cengage.com/region**.

Cengage Learning products are represented in Canada by Nelson Education, Ltd.

Visit NGL online at **ngl.cengage.com**.

Visit out corporate website at **cengage.com**.

Printed in the United States of America
1 2 3 4 5 6 7 8 19 18 17 16 15 14 13

Contents

Scope and Sequence

Unit	Writing	Grammar for Writing	Building Better Vocabulary	Original Student Writing
1 p. 2 UNDERSTANDING SENTENCE BASICS	• What Is a Sentence? • Capitalization and Punctuation in a Sentence • Editing Your Writing • Journal Writing	• Parts of a Sentence: Subjects, Verbs, and Objects • A Fragment—An Incomplete Sentence • The Verb *Be* • Prepositions of Place— *At, On,* and *In*	• Word Associations • Using Collocations • Parts of Speech	**Original Student Writing:** Write about a country you want to visit. **Photo Topic:** Can you write about a place that is important to you?
2 p. 32 UNDERSTANDING PARAGRAPH BASICS	• What Is a Paragraph? • Parts of a Paragraph: The Topic Sentence • Parts of a Paragraph: The Body • Parts of a Paragraph: The Concluding Sentence	• Using Adjectives • Word Order: Adjective + Noun • Word Order: *Be* + Adjective • Word Order: Linking Verb + Adjective • Subject Pronouns • Object Pronouns • Possessive Adjectives	• Word Associations • Using Collocations • Parts of Speech	**Original Student Writing:** Write about an interesting person that you know. **Photo Topic:** Can you describe an activity or hobby that you enjoy?
3 p. 70 WRITING ABOUT THE PRESENT	• Writing about the Present	• The Simple Present Tense: Statements • *There Is / There Are* • The Simple Present Tense: Negative Statements • Simple Sentences • Compound Sentences • Connecting Words in Compound Sentences • Using *A* and *An* with Count Nouns	• Word Associations • Using Collocations • Parts of Speech	**Original Student Writing:** Write about your favorite sport. **Photo Topic:** Can you write about things you do every day? **Timed Writing Topic:** Describe a typical "free day."

Unit	Writing	Grammar for Writing	Building Better Vocabulary	Original Student Writing
4 p. 98 **WRITING ABOUT THE PAST**	• Writing about the Past	• The Simple Past Tense of *Be* • The Simple Past Tense of Regular Verbs • The Simple Past Tense of Irregular Verbs • Time Phrases with the Simple Past Tense • The Simple Past Tense of *Be*: Negatives • The Simple Past Tense: Negatives • Using *But* Correctly • Sentence Variety: Complex Sentences • Using Complex Sentences to Show Time Order	• Word Associations • Using Collocations • Parts of Speech	**Original Student Writing:** Write about an important person. **Photo Topic:** Can you write about the home you lived in as a child? **Timed Writing Topic:** Describe an event or time from your past.
5 p. 128 **DESCRIBING ACTIONS**	• Describing Actions	• The Present Progressive Tense • Verbs in Complex Sentences • Adverbs of Manner • Prepositional Phrases of Place	• Word Associations • Using Collocations • Parts of Speech	**Original Student Writing:** Write about what is happening in an emergency situation. **Photo Topic:** Can you write about what is happening at this moment? **Timed Writing Topic:** Describe an activity that you are doing this year.
6 p. 152 **WRITING ABOUT THE FUTURE**	• Writing about the Future	• The Simple Future Tense: *Be Going To* • The Simple Future Tense: *Will* • Time Words and Phrases • The Simple Future Tense: Negatives • Verbs in Complex Sentences about the Future • The Indefinite Articles: *A/An* • The Definite Article: *The* • Article Use Summary • Using Modifiers with Singular Count Nouns • Complex Sentences with *Because*	• Word Associations • Using Collocations • Parts of Speech	**Original Student Writing:** Write about an event in your future. **Photo Topic:** Can you write about what you think will happen in the future? **Timed Writing Topic:** Describe something that you plan to do next year.

Unit	Writing	Grammar for Writing	Building Better Vocabulary	Original Student Writing
7 p. 180 **WRITING COMPLEX SENTENCES WITH ADJECTIVE CLAUSES**	• The Importance of Sentence Variety	• Sentence Variety: Recognizing Sentences with Adjective Clauses • Sentence Variety: Writing Adjective Clauses • Using Modals to Add Meaning	• Word Associations • Using Collocations • Parts of Speech	**Original Student Writing:** Write about your dining preference: cooking at home vs. eating out. **Photo Topic:** Can you write about someone or something you like? **Timed Writing Topic:** Describe something that is important to you.
8 p. 206 **PULLING IT ALL TOGETHER AND PREPARING FOR MORE**	• Review: Parts of a Paragraph • Brief Reader Response: Writing a Response to Topics in the News	• Writer's Note: Making Your Writing More Interesting • Verbs that Express an Opinion • Writer's Note: Using *Should* to Soften Your Tone	• Word Associations • Using Collocations • Parts of Speech	**Original Student Writing:** Write your opinion on banning smoking in public places. Write your opinion on government limits on the size of sugary drinks. **Photo Topic:** Can you write about a type of art that you feel strongly about?

Overview

Framed by engaging **National Geographic** images, the new edition of the *Great Writing* series helps students write better sentences, paragraphs, and essays. The new *Foundations* level meets the needs of low-level learners through basic vocabulary development and spelling practice, and all levels feature clear explanations applied directly to appropriate practice opportunities. The new edition of the *Great Writing* series develops academic writing skills for learners at all levels.

> *Great Writing: Foundations* focuses on basic sentence construction, emphasizing grammar, vocabulary, spelling, and composition.

> *Great Writing 1* focuses on sentences as they appear in paragraphs.

> *Great Writing 2* teaches paragraph development.

> *Great Writing 3* transitions from paragraphs to essays.

> *Great Writing 4* focuses on essays.

> *Great Writing 5* practices more advanced essays.

The earliest ESL composition textbooks were merely extensions of ESL grammar classes. The activities in these books did not practice English composition as much as they did ESL grammar points. Later books, on the other hand, tended to focus too much on the composing process. We feel that this focus ignores the important fact that the real goal for English learners is both to produce a presentable product and to understand the composing process. From our years of ESL and other L2 teaching experience, we believe that the *Great Writing* series allows English learners to achieve this goal.

Great Writing 1: Great Sentences for Great Paragraphs offers introductory material on writing correct sentences within simple paragraphs. The book is designed for high-beginning to low intermediate-students. Depending on the class level and the amount of writing that is done outside of class, there is enough material for 60 to 80 classroom hours. If a more substantial amount of writing is done outside of class, the number of hours for a faster group can be as few as 50.

Organization

In *Great Writing 1*, Units 1 and 2 provide an overview of basic sentence and paragraph structure. Units 3 through 7 focus on helping students to write syntactically correct sentences within the framework of five commonly taught grammatical structures. While it is not necessary to cover these five points in their given order, the current sequencing allows for recycling of grammatical, syntactical, and lexical items. Unit 8 is now a streamlined review unit that provides additional guided and free writing practice based on learning objectives from Units 1 to 7. The *Brief Writer's Handbook* provides additional reference material, while the Appendices contain extra practice material to support both the process and the mechanics of writing.

Contents of a Unit

Although each unit has specific writing objectives (listed at the beginning of the unit), the following features appear in every unit:

Example Paragraphs

Because we believe that writing and reading are inextricably related, the 74 example paragraphs model a grammar or sentence structure and/or provide editing activities. Models are often followed by questions about organization, syntactic structures, or other composition features. New, potentially unfamiliar vocabulary words are glossed on the side of each paragraph. These words can provide students with a list of vocabulary to add to a separate vocabulary notebook.

Grammar for Writing

Since good writing requires knowledge of the mechanics of English, *Great Writing 1* includes clear charts and detailed instruction that relates directly to the writing assignments. In addition, numerous activities give students the opportunity to practice and refine their grammar and writing knowledge and skills.

Activities

The new, fourth edition contains 184 activities. In addition, there are 80 suggestions for additional paragraph writing assignments found in the units. These writing, grammar, and vocabulary activities gradually build the skills students need to write well-crafted sentences and simple paragraphs, and provide learners with more input in English composition and paragraph organization and cohesion.

Building Better Vocabulary

Each unit includes three vocabulary-building activities to build schema and collocations. In the first activity, *Word Associations*, the student identifies words that best relate to the target vocabulary word. This allows them to build connections to more words and thus grow their vocabulary more quickly. Words from the Academic Word List are starred (see page 245 for the complete list). The second activity, *Using Collocations*, helps students learn specific word combinations, or collocations, which will help their original writing sound more advanced. It is helpful to encourage students to use these new words in their Original Student Writing assignment and to add them to a vocabulary notebook. In the final activity, *Parts of Speech,* students study suffixes and parts of speech. Understanding how suffixes are related to the different parts of speech allows students to expand their understanding of word formation in English, giving them a broader vocabulary base and a better understanding of word order for better writing skills.

Writer's Notes

Great Writing 1: Great Sentences for Great Paragraphs features small pieces of writing advice that help writers understand more about use and format. Content includes word choice, building sentence variety, peer editing guidelines, and tips on common academic writing conventions.

Building Better Sentences

Towards the end of Units 1–7, students are asked to turn to Appendix 1 and work on building better sentences. Each practice is intentionally short and includes only three problems. In each problem, there are two to five short sentences that the students must combine into a single sentence that expresses all the ideas in a logical and grammatically correct manner.

Original Writing

Each unit includes an activity that requires students to do some form of writing. Original Student Writing includes writing prompts and a set of directions to encourage students to follow the writing process and refer back to the lessons taught in the unit.

Additional Writing Topics give students the opportunity to continue practicing their writing skills. The first topic links back to the opening photograph and writing prompt. It is up to the teacher to decide whether all students will write about the same topic or whether each student is free to choose any of the topics listed.

Peer Editing

At the end of each unit, a peer editing activity offers students the opportunity to provide written comments to one another with the goal of improving their simple paragraphs. A unique peer editing sheet for each unit can be found online at NGL.Cengage.com. Each one provides the guidance and structure that is necessary for students at this level to perform this task with success. We recommend that students spend 15 to 20 minutes reading a classmate's paragraph and writing comments using the questions on the peer editing sheet.

Timed Writing

One way to improve students' comfort level with the task of writing under a deadline, such as during a testing situation, is to provide them with numerous writing opportunities that are timed. The final activity in Units 3 through 7 features a timed-writing prompt that is geared toward the grammar and sentence structure presented in that unit. Students are given five minutes to read the prompt and make a quick writing plan, followed by 20 minutes of actual writing. Instructors may use this activity at any time during the lesson.

What's New in This Edition?

- Engaging images from **National Geographic** connect learning to the greater world.
- New and updated readings act as springboards and models for writing.
- Updated Grammar for Writing sections clearly present grammar and help students learn the structures for writing.
- Streamlined instruction and practice activities offer step-by-step guidelines to focus writers on both the writing process and product.
- Words from the Academic Word List are highlighted in vocabulary activities, encouraging students to expand their word knowledge.
- The expanded *Brief Writer's Handbook* now includes a Useful Vocabulary for Writing section to help writers choose appropriate language for the different rhetorical modes.
- An all-new level, *Great Writing: Foundations* introduces students to the basics of grammar, spelling, and vocabulary.
- A new Online Workbook encourages learners to further practice grammar, vocabulary, and editing skills. Students can also write paragraphs or essays, and submit them to the instructor electronically.
- An updated Presentation Tool allows instructors to use the book in an interactive whiteboard setting and demonstrate the editing process.
- An eBook provides another option to use *Great Writing* in a traditional or blended learning environment.

Ancillary Components

In addition to the *Great Writing 1: Great Sentences for Great Paragraphs* Student Book, the following components help both the instructor and the students expand their learning and teaching.

- **Online Workbook at NGL.Cengage.com/GW1**: Includes a wealth of vocabulary, grammar, writing, and editing practice with immediate feedback.
- **Classroom Presentation Tool CD-ROM**: Offers instructors the ability to lead whole-class presentations and demonstrate the editing process.
- **Assessment CD-ROM with ExamView®**: Allows instructors to create and customize tests.
- **Online Teacher's Notes**: Help instructors prepare lessons and teach effectively.
- **Online Answer Key**: Provides answers to every activity.
- **eBook**: Offers an interactive option.

Inside a Unit
Great Writing 1: Great Sentences for Great Paragraphs

Framed by engaging *National Geographic* content, the new edition of the *Great Writing* series helps students write better sentences, paragraphs, and essays. *Great Writing* develops academic writing skills for learners at all levels through clear explanations applied directly to appropriate practice opportunities.

Impactful **National Geographic** images provide engaging topics to encourage student writing.

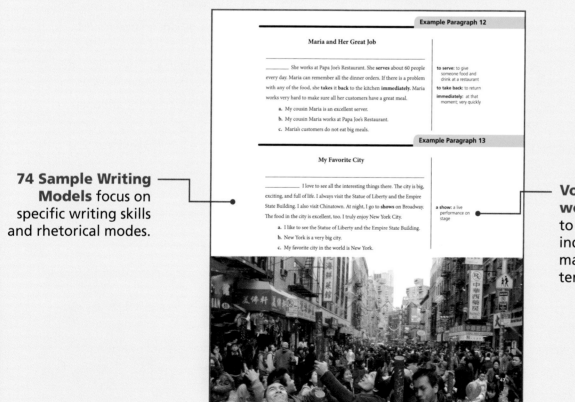

74 Sample Writing Models focus on specific writing skills and rhetorical modes.

Vocabulary words are glossed to encourage independent mastery of new terms.

Inside a Unit

Great Writing 1: Great Sentences for Great Paragraphs

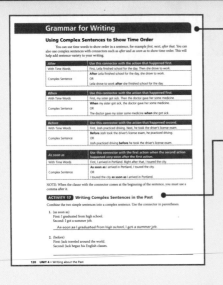

New **Grammar for Writing** sections provide clear explanations and examples, giving learners easy access to the structures they will use in their writing.

Guided, structured activities help students practice writing, grammar, and editing skills.

Building Better Vocabulary

ACTIVITY 23 Word Associations

Circle the word or phrase that is most closely related to the word or phrase on the left. If necessary, use a dictionary to check the meaning of words you do not know.

	A	B
1. an opinion	a belief	a fact
2. a headache	pain	relaxation
3. to consider	to talk to	to think about
4. to spend	money comes in	money goes out
5. historic	career	city
6. furniture	a rug	a sofa

Building Better Vocabulary activities highlight words from the Academic Word List and prompt students to apply their vocabulary and knowledge of collocations.

Original Student Writing

ACTIVITY 26 Original Writing Practice

Follow these instructions.

- Answer the questions about an interesting person that you know. Use a complete sentence for each answer. Put a check (✓) next to each question as you answer it.
- As you write, use at least two of the vocabulary words or phrases presented in Activity 23, Activity 24, and Activity 25 in your sentences. Underline these words and phrases in your sentences.
- Copy your sentences into a paragraph on the lines provided on page 67.
- Use the checklist on page 68 to edit your work.

_____ 1. Who is the most interesting person you know?

_____ 2. How do you know this person?

_____ 3. Why is this person interesting? List three reasons why this person is so interesting. Give an example to support each reason. (Use adjectives in your descriptions.)

Original Student Writing includes topics and prompts to encourage students to combine the grammar, vocabulary, and writing lessons in personal assignments.

Peer Editing activities increase student awareness of common errors.

Timed Writing

How quickly can you write in English? There are many times when you must write quickly, such as on a test. It is important to feel comfortable during those times. Timed-writing practice can make you feel better about writing quickly in English.

1. Take out a piece of paper.
2. Read the writing prompt below.
3. Brainstorm ideas for five minutes.
4. Write eight to ten sentences.
5. You have 20 minutes to write.

Describe a sad (or happy, frightening, funny, important, etc.) event or time from your past. What was the event or time? Give examples of how this event or time made you feel that emotion.

Timed Writing activities prepare students for success on standardized and international writing exams.

The **Brief Writer's Handbook** includes many resources for the developing writer, including a new Useful Vocabulary for Better Writing section.

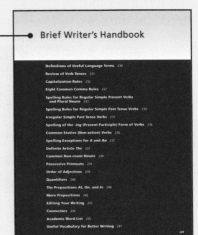

Brief Writer's Handbook

Technology *Great Writing 1*

For Instructors:

The NEW Presentation Tool CD-ROM makes instruction clearer and learning easier through editing activities, sentence-building activities, and grammar presentations.

Teacher's Notes available on the *Great Writing* website include teaching suggestions for each activity, Peer Editing sheets, and answer key for activities in the Student Book.

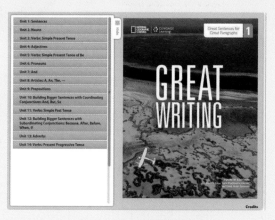

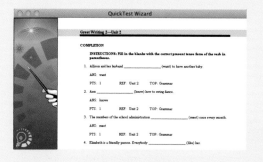

The Assessment CD-ROM with Exam*View*® allows instructors to create and customize tests and quizzes easily.

For Students:

The Online Workbook: Each level features additional independent practice in vocabulary, grammar, writing, and editing.

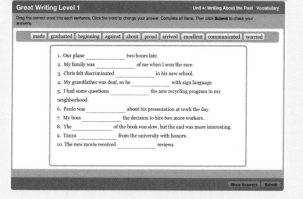

Great Writing eBooks are available at all levels and are compatible with iPads, laptops, and smart phones.

Acknowledgements

We would like to thank the hundreds of ESL and English composition colleagues who have generously shared their ideas, insights, and feedback on second language writing, university English course requirements, and textbook design.

We would also like to thank Laura Le Dréan, Thomas Jefferies, Ian Martin, and Emily Stewart from National Geographic Learning for their guidance. We are extremely grateful for the support given to us by our developmental editors Katherine Carroll, Charlotte Sturdy, and Yeny Kim. We also remain forever grateful to our previous editors at Houghton Mifflin, Susan Maguire, Kathy Sands-Boehmer, and Kathleen Smith, for their indispensable guidance throughout the birth and growth of this writing project.

Likewise, we are indebted to the following reviewers who offered ideas and suggestions that shaped our revisions:

Barbara Smith-Palinkas, Hillsborough Community College, Florida
Laura Taylor, Iowa State University, Iowa
Mary Barratt, Iowa State University, Iowa
Abdelhay Belfakir, University of Central Florida, Florida
Taoufik Ferjani, Zayed University, United Arab Emirates
Cheryl Acorn, Pasadena City College, California
Paul McGarry, Santa Barbara City College, California
Fernanda Ortiz, University of Arizona, Arizona
Michelle Jeffries, University of Arkansas—Fayetteville, Arkansas
Suzanne Medina, California State University—Dominguez Hills, California
Kristi Miller, American English Institute, California
Kevin Van Houten, Glendale Community College, California
Izabella Kojic-Sabo, University of Windsor, Canada
Wayne Fong, Aston School, China
Yiwei Shu, New Oriental School, China
Raul Billini, John F. Kennedy Institute of Languages, Dominican Republic
Rosa Vasquez, John F. Kennedy Institute of Languages, Dominican Republic
Mike Sfiropoulos, Palm Beach State College, Florida
Louise Gobron, Georgia State University, Georgia
Gabriella Cambiasso, City College of Chicago—Harold Washington, Illinois
Lin Cui, Harper College, Illinois
Laura Aoki, Kurume University, Japan
Rieko Ashida, Konan University, Japan
Greg Holloway, Kyushu Institute of Technology, Japan
Collin James, Kansai Gaigo University, Japan
Lindsay Mack, Ritsumeikan Asia Pacific University, Japan
Robert Staehlin, Morioka University, Japan
Jenny Selvidge, Donnelly College, Kansas
Phan Vongphrachanh, Donnelly College, Kansas
Virginia Van Hest Bastaki, Kuwait University, Kuwait
Jennifer Jakubic, Century College, Minnesota
Trina Goslin, University of Nevada—Reno, Nevada
Margaret Layton, University of Nevada—Reno, Nevada
Amy Metcalf, University of Nevada—Reno, Nevada
Gail Fernandez, Bergen Community College, New Jersey

Lynn Meng, Union County College—Elizabeth, New Jersey
Zoe Isaacson, Queens College, New York
Sherwin Kizner, Queens College, New York
Linnea Spitzer, Portland State University, Oregon
Jennifer Stenseth, Portland State University, Oregon
Rebecca Valdovinos, Oregon State University, Oregon
Renata Ruff, Prince Mohammed University, Saudi Arabia
Ya Li Chao, National Taichung University of Science and Technology, Taiwan
Kuei-ping Hsu, National Tsing Hua University, Taiwan
Morris Huang, National Taiwan University of Science and Technology, Taiwan
Cheng-Che Lin, Tainan University of Technology, Taiwan
Rita Yeh, Chia Nan University of Pharmacy and Science, Taiwan
Nguyen Chanh Tri, Vietnam Australia International School, Vietnam
Mai Minh Tien, Vietnam Australia International School, Vietnam
Tuan Nguyen, Vietnam Australia International School, Vietnam
Nguyen Thi Thanh The, Vietnam Australia International School, Vietnam
Nguyen Vu Minh Phuong, Vietnam Australia International School, Vietnam
Colleen Comidy, Seattle Central Community College, Washington
Cindy Etter, University of Washington, Washington
Kris Hardy, Seattle Central Community College, Washington
Liese Rajesh, Seattle Central Community College, Washington

Finally, many thanks go to the thousands of our students who have taught us throughout our teaching careers what ESL/EFL composition ought to be. Without them, this work would have been impossible.

Keith S. Folse
April Muchmore-Vokoun
Elena Vestri Solomon

Photo Credits

Understanding Sentence Basics

A ride on the London Eye provides a clear view over the city, including the Palace of Westminster.

OBJECTIVES   To learn how to write correct simple sentences
To learn about subjects, verbs, and objects
To practice the verb *be* and prepositions of place
To practice correct capitalization and punctuation
To understand editing and journaling

Can you describe an amazing place?

What Is a Sentence?

A **sentence** is a group of words that expresses a complete thought. For example:

Joe likes basketball.

The weather is cold today.

Words can go together to make sentences. Sentences can go together to make a paragraph. Finally, paragraphs can be combined into an essay. In this book, you will study sentences and sentences in paragraphs.

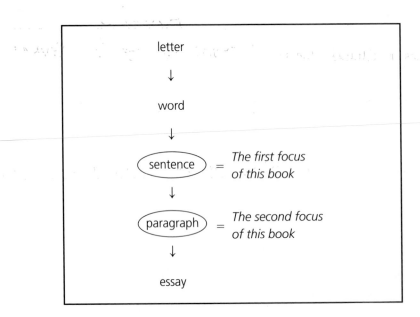

Do You Know?

Do you know what languages the sentences on the right are in? Check your answers on the bottom of page 31.

The class has twelve students.

The student is from Canada.

Mike speaks French and English.

A cat has a tail and four legs.

We want to learn English.

Ci sono dodici studenti nella classe.

這位學生是來自加拿大。

Miklós beszél franciául és angolul.

Pisica are o coadă şi patru picioare.

نريد ان نتعلم الانجليزية

ACTIVITY 1 **Changing Words into Sentences**

Unscramble the words to make correct sentences.

1. My name / Angela / is / . _My name is Angela._

2. from Kearney, Nebraska / I / am / . I am from Kearney Nebraska

3. in the middle of the United States / a small city / Kearney / is / . Kearney is a small city in the middle of the united states

4. have / two parents / I / . I have two parents

5. have / and one sister / I / three brothers / . I have three brothers and one sister

6. like to ride / I / horses/ . I like to ride horses

7. in the country / like to hike / I / . I like to hike in the country.

5

8. am / I / an / English teacher / . *I am an English teacher*

9. foreign languages / like to study / I / . *I like to study foreign languages*

10. like / I / my job / very much / . *I like my job very much*

ACTIVITY 2 Writing Simple Sentences

A. Write six to ten sentences about yourself. Follow the examples in Activity 1.

1. *I am a girl*
2. *I like to read.*
3. *I have one sister and two brother*
4. *I like history*
5. _____
6. _____
7. _____
8. _____
9. _____
10. _____

B. Read your sentences to a classmate. Then your classmate will read his / her sentences to you. Write four things you learned about your classmate.

1. _____
2. _____
3. _____
4. _____

Grammar for Writing

Parts of a Sentence: Subjects, Verbs, and Objects

In this unit, you will learn about a sentence pattern that we call a **simple sentence**. In English, every sentence has two main parts: the subject and the verb. Sometimes there is an object and/or other information after the verb.

Subject	Verb	(Object)	(Other Information)
Maria	sings.		
She	plays	the piano.	
Maria	practices		at home.
She	sings	songs	in the morning.

Subject

The **subject** is the person or thing that does the action. The subject:

- can be a noun or a pronoun
- can be two (or more) nouns / pronouns. However, the nouns / pronouns must share the same verb(s).

    Maria and her sister go to piano class every week.

Verb

The **verb** tells what the subject is doing. The verb:

- is usually an action word, such as *go, speak, write, swim,* and *watch*
- sometimes does not have much action, such as *be* (*am, is, are, was, were*), *like, want,* and *need*
- can have two (or more) actions for one subject

    They **create** and **play** beautiful music.

Object

The **object** is the thing or person after the main verb. The object:

- receives the action of the verb
- can be a noun or a pronoun
- can be two (or more) nouns / pronouns

    Maria's brother plays **guitar** and **violin.**

Other Information

Sentences can contain other information after the verb and the object, such as time words / phrases or place phrases. When a sentence has a time word / phrase and a place phrase, the time word / phrase usually comes last.

place   time word/
phrase   phrase

Maria and her sister practice the piano **at home every day.**

ACTIVITY 3 Identifying Subjects, Verbs, and Objects

Read these sentences about making tuna salad. Underline each subject. Circle each verb. Put a box around any objects.

1. Tuna salad (is) easy to make.

2. The ingredients (are) simple and cheap.

3. Two ingredients (are) tuna fish and mayonnaise.

4. I also use onions, salt, and pepper.

5. First, I cut up the onion.

6. Then I add the tuna fish and the mayonnaise.

7. Finally, I add some salt and a lot of pepper.

8. Without a doubt, tuna salad is my favorite food!

ACTIVITY 4 Unscrambling Sentences

Unscramble the words to make correct sentences.

1. in Central America / a small country / Costa Rica / is / .

   Costa Rica is a small Country in central America

2. between Panama / and Nicaragua / It / is / .

   It is between Panama and Nicaragua

3. This country / between the Pacific Ocean / is / and the Caribbean Sea / .

   This country is between the Pacific Ocean
   and the caribbean sea.

4. more than four million / is / The population / of Costa Rica / .

   The population of Costa Rica is more
   than four million

5. Many tourists / there / go / .

Many tourists go there

6. wild animals / They / all the time / see / in the jungle / .

They all the time see in the Junste wild animals

7. is / in the world / the most beautiful country / It / .

It is the most beautiful Country in the world.

8. hope to visit / one day / I / this beautiful country / .

I hope to visit one day this beautiful country

ACTIVITY 5 Using Subject-Verb Word Order in a Paragraph

Fill in the missing subjects and verbs from the word bank for each blank. You will use some words more than once. Some blanks can have more than one answer.

Caroline	she	her lunch break	Anderson Supermarket	has	~~is~~
wakes up	~~starts~~	attends	likes	~~enjoys~~	works

Example Paragraph 1

A Great Place to Work

1 _____ a great job at Anderson Supermarket. **2** _____ there on Monday, Tuesday, and Thursday. She does not go to work there on Wednesday because **3** _____ classes at Jefferson Community College. On her workdays, **4** ____ *is* ____ at 6 A.M. **5** ____ *starts* ____ her workday at 8 A.M.

6 _____ from 8 A.M. to 5 P.M.

7 _____ from 12:30 to 1:30.

8 ____ *enjoys* ____ her job very much.

9 _____ her coworkers, too. For Caroline,

10 _____ a great place to work.

9

Grammar for Writing

A Fragment—An Incomplete Sentence

Every sentence must have a subject and a verb. A sentence without a subject or without a verb is called a **fragment**. A fragment is a piece of a sentence. It is not a complete sentence.

✗ John is my brother. <u>Works</u> at Ames Bank. (no subject)

✓ John is my brother. He works at Ames Bank.

✗ Many <u>people</u> a white car. (no verb)

✓ Many people have a white car.

In writing, a fragment is a serious mistake. When you write, check each sentence to make sure that there is a subject <u>and</u> a verb.

ACTIVITY 6 **Editing: Sentence or Fragment?**

Identify each group of words as a fragment (*F*) or a complete sentence (*S*). Then add the missing part of the sentence to the fragments to make them complete sentences.

1. _____S_____ Hans lives in a big apartment.

2. _____F_____ My mother ^makes breakfast every morning.

3. _____F_____ Is incredibly delicious.

4. _____S_____ Karen has a car.

5. _____F_____ They *are* my cousins from Miami.

6. _____F_____ You *are* a student.

7. _____S_____ Michael likes classical music.

8. _____F_____ Nicole and Jean *are* very best friends.

9. _____S_____ The girls play soccer after school.

10. _____S_____ I am from Colombia.

Grammar for Writing

The Verb *Be*

The most frequently used verb in the English language is the verb **be**. *Be* has five main forms: *am, is, are, was,* and *were.*

I **am** a student. My writing **is** good. My classes **are** difficult.

I **was** a good student in kindergarten. The assignments **were** easy.

There are four common sentence patterns for *be*.

Subject	+	Be	+	Adjective
I		am		happy.

Subject	+	Be	+	Noun
Ceviche		is		a seafood dish.

Subject	+	Be	+	Place Phrase
My keys		are		on the table.

When you begin a sentence with *there,* the subject follows the verb *be*.

There	+	Be	+	Subject	+	(Extra information: usually place or time)
There		is		a beautiful painting		on the wall.
There		were		two empty plates		on the table this morning.
There		was		a big meeting		at our company last week.

ACTIVITY 7 Identifying Subjects and Verbs

Underline the subjects and circle the verbs in the paragraph.

Example Paragraph 2

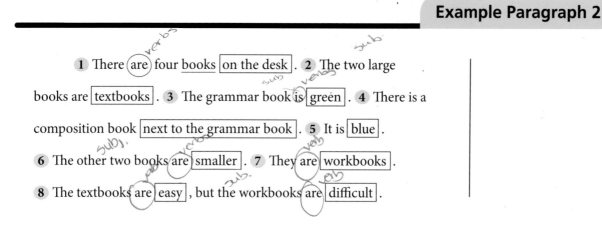

1 There (are) four books on the desk . **2** The two large books are textbooks . **3** The grammar book is green . **4** There is a composition book next to the grammar book . **5** It is blue . **6** The other two books are smaller . **7** They are workbooks . **8** The textbooks are easy , but the workbooks are difficult .

ACTIVITY 8 · Identifying Words and Phrases

Look at the sentences in Activity 7. Identify the words or phrases in boxes as an *adjective*, a *noun*, or a *place phrase*.

1. on the desk = _place phrase_

2. textbooks = _noun_

3. green = _adjective_

4. next to the grammar book = _place phrase_

5. blue = _adjetive_

6. smaller = _adjetive_

7. workbooks = _noun_

8. easy = _adjetive_

9. difficult = _adjetive_

ACTIVITY 9 · Completing Sentences with *Be*

Complete each sentence with the correct form of *be*. Then write two more sentences about the topic using the common sentence patterns with *be*.

1. There ___are___ seven colors in a rainbow. _These colors are red, orange, yellow,_

   green, blue, indigo, and violet. My favorite rainbow color is green.

2. There _____are_____ twenty-six letters in the English alphabet. _____

_____

_____

3. There _____are_____ different students in my class. _____

_____

_____

4. There _____is_____ an insect on the window. _____

_____

_____

5. There _____is_____ a huge map of the world on the wall in our classroom. _____

_____

_____

6. There _____are_____ many different animals in a zoo. _____

_____

_____

Grammar for Writing

Prepositions of Place—*At, On,* and *In*

Three important **prepositions** are *at, on,* and *in*. These prepositions are often used to describe location.

The pyramid design shows the difference in meaning between *at, on,* and *in.*

- The top of the pyramid is a small, specific place. We use *at* for a specific location or building, such as business names and street addresses (number + street.)

- The middle of the pyramid is larger than the top. We use *on* for a street name, which is larger than a specific place like a bank or specific address.

- The bottom of the pyramid is the largest. We use *in* for a city, state, region, or country—places that are much larger than a street.

AT
at Union Bank
at 335 Main Street

ON
on Main Street

IN
in Orlando
in Florida
in the United States

There is a list of common time prepositions on pages 240–242 in the *Brief Writer's Handbook.*

Choosing the Correct Preposition

Fill in each blank with the correct preposition. Use *at, on,* or *in.*

1. The Sahara is a desert region _____in_____ Africa.

2. My friend Tina works _____in (at)_____ Washington Central Bank.

3. The Eiffel Tower is a famous landmark _____in_____ Paris.

4. There is a very popular sushi restaurant _____on_____ Pine Street.

5. Busan is an interesting city _____in_____ South Korea.

6. My friends and I attend classes _____at_____ a local university _____in_____ our city.

7. There are many theaters _____on_____ Broadway Avenue _____in_____ New York.

8. The company meeting will be _____at_____ 1202 Waters Avenue.

Choosing the Correct Preposition

Circle the correct prepositions.

Example Paragraph 3

Banks in a Small Town

It is surprising that Nelson has seven banks. Nelson is a small town (**1.** at / on / (in)) California. There are only about 36,000 people (**2.** at / on / (in)) this town. However, there are three banks, and each bank has at least two branches. The banks are National, First California, and Trust. National Bank has branches (**3.** (at) / on / in) 60 Green Street and (**4.** at / (on) / in) Hanks Avenue. First California Bank has branches (**5.** at / (on) / in) Princeton Street and (**6.** at / (on) / in) Lee Road. Trust Bank has branches (**7.** at / on / in) 27 Temple Street, (**8.** at / (on) / in) Whispering Street, and (**9.** (at) / on / in) 445 Orange Avenue. No one understands why there are seven banks (**10.** at / on / (in)) a small town like Nelson, California.

Capitalization and Punctuation in a Sentence

In addition to having a subject and verb, a correct sentence must have correct capitalization and punctuation.

Beginning a Sentence with a Capital Letter

In English, there are two kinds of letters: **capital letters** (*H, R*) and **lowercase letters** (*h, r*).

CAPITAL LETTERS	A B C D E F G H I J K L M N O P Q R S T U V W X Y Z
lowercase letters	a b c d e f g h i j k l m n o p q r s t u v w x y z

Most of the time, we use lowercase letters. However, we <u>always</u> begin a sentence with a CAPITAL letter.

  ✗ the boxes on the table are heavy.

  ✓ The boxes on the table are heavy.

  ✗ where do you live?

  ✓ Where do you live?

Ending a Sentence with a Period

The most common way to end a sentence is with a **period** (.).

  ✗ Brazil is a large country (no period)

  ✓ Brazil is a large country.

  ✗ I do not like coffee with sugar (no period)

  ✓ I do not like coffee with sugar.

ACTIVITY 12 **Practicing Capitalization and Punctuation**

Unscramble the words to write simple sentences. Use correct capitalization and punctuation.

1. spaghetti / most kids / like

most kids like spaghetti

2. enjoy / they / the taste of spaghetti

they enjoy the taste of spaghetti

3. tomato sauce / on their spaghetti / some kids / put

Some kids put on their

4. the color of spaghetti with the sauce / they / love

they love the color of spaghetti with the sauce

5. like / on their spaghetti / cheese / other kids

other kids like cheese on their spaghetti.

6. love to eat / most kids / spaghetti

most kids love to eat spaghetti

Writing Simple Sentences

Copy the sentences you unscrambled in Activity 12. In each sentence, change the word *spaghetti* to *ice cream*. Also change *most kids* to *Erika and Zahra*. Make other appropriate vocabulary changes as necessary.

1. _____

2. _____

3. _____

4. _____

5. _____

6. _____

Capital Letters for Proper Nouns

A **proper noun** is a specific person, place, or thing. A proper noun always begins with a capital letter.

Proper Noun	Examples
A Specific Person	✗ One famous person in history is nelson mandela.
	✓ One famous person in history is Nelson Mandela.
A Specific Place	✗ My favorite city is new york city.
	✓ My favorite city is New York City.
A Specific Thing	✗ Paco watched the movie *slumdog millionaire* last night.
	✓ Paco watched the movie *Slumdog Millionaire* last night.
Days and Months	✗ The first sunday of july is an important day to me.
	✓ The first Sunday of July is an important day to me.
Languages and Countries	✗ In india, the most common languages are hindi and english.
	✓ In India, the most common languages are Hindi and English.

There is a complete list of capitalization rules on page 232 in the *Brief Writer's Handbook.*

Editing Simple Sentences

In each sentence, correct the capitalization mistake(s) and add a period at the end. Then write the sentences on another piece of paper.

1. my cousin albert has an interesting job.

2. he is a taxi driver in chicago

3. albert owns his own taxi company

4. it is called lightning taxi service

5. albert drives a taxi every day except Sunday

6. may and june are busy months for albert

7. tourists from canada and europe often use albert's company

8. he drives his passengers to interesting locations

9. he often sees the john hancock observatory, millennium park, and wrigley field

10. my cousin practices english with his customers

11. albert loves his job

Ending a Sentence with a Question Mark or Exclamation Point

Not all sentences end with a period. Some sentences are questions, and they end with a **question mark (?)**. Writers do not use question marks very often in academic writing.

✗ Is Brazil a large country.

✓ Is Brazil a large country?

✗ Where do you live.

✓ Where do you live?

Some sentences end with an **exclamation point** (!) to show emphasis or emotion. Exclamation points are rarely used in formal academic writing. However, when a sentence expresses surprise or strong emotion, it is appropriate to use an exclamation point.

Simple fact: It is snowing.

With surprise: It is snowing!

Simple fact: My sister had a baby last night.

With surprise: My sister had a baby last night!

Identifying Statements, Questions, and Exclamations

Identify each sentence as a statement (*S*), question (*Q*), or exclamation (*E*). Then add the correct punctuation to the end of the sentence.

1. ___Q___ How many days are in a month?

2. ___S___ The answer depends on the month.

3. ___S___ Only four months have 30 days

4. ___S___ An example of a month with only 30 days is September

5. ___S___ Other months have 31 days

6. ___S___ Examples of months with 31 days are July and December

7. ___Q___ Which month never has 30 days

8. ___S___ The answer is February

9. ___S___ February usually has only 28 days

10. ___S___ All my brothers and sisters were born in the first two weeks of February

○	FEBRUARY					○
Sun	Mon	Tue	Wed	Thu	Fri	Sat
						1
2	3	4	5	6	7	8
9	10	11	12	13	14	15
16	17	18	19	20	21	22
23	24	25	26	27	28	

Taking a World Quiz

Unscramble the words to write questions. Then write the answers in complete sentences. Check for correct word order. Use correct capitalization and end punctuation.

1. what / the capital / of brazil / is

   Question: _What is the capital of Brazil?_

   Answer: _The capital of Brazil is Brasilia._

2. is / what city / the white house in

   Question: _What city is in the white house?_

   Answer: _Washington_

3. what / in mexico / the biggest city / is

   Question: _What is the bigges city in mexico?_

   Answer: _____

4. the eiffel tower in / what city / is

   Question: _What city is in the eiffel tower in_

   Answer: _____

5. what continent / the nile river in / is

Question: What continent is in the nile river in?

Answer: _____

6. the andes mountains / are / where

Question: Where are the andes mountains?

Answer: _____

7. is / what / the capital of saudi arabia

Question: what is the capital of sadi arabia?

Answer: _____

8. in canada / what / the biggest province / is

Question: what is the bisses province in canada?

Answer: _____

3/24

Rewrite the questions using correct capitalization and end punctuation. Then ask a classmate the questions. (Choose a DIFFERENT partner from the one you used in Activity 2.) Write your classmate's answers in complete sentences. Use correct capitalization and punctuation.

1. what is your name

   Question: My name is cristina

   Answer: _____

2. where are you from

   Question: I am from Puerto Rico

   Answer: _____

3. where do you live

   Question: I live in Boston.

   Answer: _____

4. how many people are in your family

   Question: In my family I have 5 people

   Answer: _____

5. do you have a car

   Question: no I don't have a Car

   Answer: _____

6. what food do you like to eat

   Question: I like to eat Crab.

   Answer: _____

7. what is your favorite place to visit

   Question: my favorite Place to visit is paris

   Answer: _____

8. what is your favorite movie

   Question: My favorite movie is Justin bieber

   Answer: _____

ACTIVITY 18 Editing: Grammar and Sentence Review

Correct the paragraph. There are 10 mistakes. The first mistake has been corrected for you.

3 capitalization mistakes
2 punctuation mistakes
1 missing subject
3 missing verbs
1 incorrect preposition

Example Paragraph 4

Making Hummus

Hummus *is* a very easy snack to make. The ingredients simple and
cheap. Chickpeas and crushed Garlic are two ingredients. I also use lemon
juice, olive oil, and salt. First, wash and mash the chickpeas at a bowl. Then
I add the crushed garlic and salt Finally, i mix in the lemon juice and olive
oil. some people add tahini paste, too? This fast treat now ready to eat.

Building Better Sentences: For further practice with the sentences and paragraphs in this unit, go to Practice 1 on page 253 in Appendix I.

Building Better Vocabulary

ACTIVITY 19 Word Associations

Circle the word or phrase that is most closely related to the word or phrase on the left. If necessary, use a dictionary to check the meaning of words you do not know.

	A	B
1. a surprise	known	unknown
2. to work	at the beach	at the office
3. to understand	to add	to know
4. ingredients	when you cook	when you read
5. simple	difficult	not difficult
6. cheap	a high price	a low price
7. finally*	the first	the last
8. to cut up	to make into many pieces	to keep in one piece
9. an addition	something put in	something taken out

10.	to attend	(to be present)	to do something
11.	a break	a short process	(a short rest)
12.	to enjoy	to dislike	(to like)
13.	a company	(a business)	a school
14.	a region*	(a place)	something you believe
15.	famous	professional	(well known)

*Words that are part of the Academic Word List. See pages 245–246 for a complete list.

ACTIVITY 20 **Using Collocations**

Fill in each blank with the word that most naturally completes the phrase on the right. If necessary, use a dictionary to check the meaning of words you do not know.

1. popular / capital   a __popular__ actor

2. to / from   to add lemon juice __to__ the hummus

3. a supermarket / a class   to attend __a class__

4. region / branch   a bank __branch__

5. result / break   a surprising __result__

6. sun / movie   an interesting __movie__

7. simple / cheap   a __simple__ answer

8. a chair / a sentence   to understand __a sentence__

9. a drink / an onion   to cut up __an onion__

10. meet / add   to __add__ salt

ACTIVITY 21   Parts of Speech

Study the word forms. Fill in each sentence with the best word form provided. Use the correct form of the verbs. If necessary, use a dictionary to check the meaning of words you do not know. (NOTE: The word in bold is the original word that appears in the unit.)

Noun	Verb	Adjective	Sentence Practice
add<u>ition</u>	**add**	addition<u>al</u>	1. She __adds__ sugar to her coffee.
			2. We plan to build an __addition__ to our home.
attend<u>ance</u>	**attend**	Ø	3. Mr. Cox checks the students' __attendance__ every day.
			4. Do you want to __attend__ the concert tomorrow?
popular<u>ity</u>	Ø	**popular**	5. Taylor is a __popular__ singer.
			6. The __popularity__ of motorcycles is incredible!
happi<u>ness</u>	Ø	**happy**	7. She is very __happy__ because it is her birthday.
			8. You cannot buy __happiness__ with money.
work	**work**	Ø	9. My sister __works__ in a supermarket.
			10. Do you enjoy your __work__?

Noun endings: *-tion, -ance, -ity, -ness*

Adjective endings: *-al, -y*

Original Student Writing

ACTIVITY 22   Original Writing Practice

Follow these instructions:

- Answer the questions, and write eight to ten complete sentences about an interesting country. Put a check (✓) next to each question as you answer it.

- As you write, use at least two vocabulary words or phrases presented in Activities 19, 20, and 21. Underline these words in your writing.

- Use the checklist on the next page to edit your sentences.

_____ 1. What country do you want to visit? _____

_____ 2. Why do you want to visit this country? _____
I want to visit Canada
Because I want to go the store of J.B

_____ 3. Where is this country located? Canada is in the
north of America

_____ **4.** How big is this country? _big_ _____

_____ **5.** What is the capital of this country? _____

_____ **6.** What is one famous monument or important place in this country? _____

_____

_____ **7.** Briefly describe this monument or place. _____

_____

_____ **8.** What do you know about food in this country? _____

_____

If you need ideas for words and phrases, see the Useful Vocabulary for Better Writing on pages 247–249.

☑ Checklist

1. ❑ I checked that each sentence has a subject and a verb.

2. ❑ I used correct capitalization and end punctuation.

3. ❑ I used *at*, *on*, and *in* correctly.

4. ❑ I checked the spelling of at least three misspelled words in a dictionary.

Editing Your Writing

Good writers need editors to help them make their writing correct. A good editor checks the grammar, spelling, and punctuation. A good editor also makes sure the writing is clear and easy to understand.

For your writing in this book, there should be two editors:

1. You. After you finish your writing, you will check your own work for mistakes.

2. A classmate. After you have edited your writing, a classmate will read your work and help you find ways to make it better.

ACTIVITY 23 Editing Simple Sentences

Some of the sentences below have mistakes with fragments, punctuation, or capitalization. Decide if the sentence is correct or incorrect, and check the appropriate box. If the sentence contains a mistake, describe the mistake. Then edit the sentence to make it correct.

1. Mexico ^is not near Great Britain.

    ❏ Correct ☑ Incorrect   Reason: fragment – missing verb

2. The Statue of Liberty is in ~~new york~~. New York

    ❏ Correct ☑ Incorrect   Reason: missing capitalization

3. Sudan is in africa.

    ☑ Correct ❏ Incorrect   Reason: Missing Capitalization

4. Portland is a popular city in Oregon.

    ☑ Correct ❏ Incorrect   Reason: N/A

5. Austria and Hungary in Europe.

    ❏ Correct ☑ Incorrect   Reason: fragment missing verb

6. Russia and Canada bigger than the United States.

    ❏ Correct ☑ Incorrect   Reason: fragment Missing verb

7. Rains a lot in Southeast Asia during the rainy season.

    ❏ Correct ☑ Incorrect   Reason: fragment – Missing verb

8. Three main groups of people live in Malaysia.

    ☑ Correct ❏ Incorrect   Reason: N/A

9. Is between Mexico and Canada.

    ❏ Correct ☑ Incorrect   Reason: fragment Missing verb

10. Nepal is north of India

    ☑ Correct ❏ Incorrect   Reason: N/A

11. Of Thailand is more than 67,000,000.

    ❏ Correct ☑ Incorrect   Reason: fragment Missing verb

12. Bolivia does not any seaports.

    ❏ Correct ☑ Incorrect   Reason: fragment Missing verb

Peer Editing

A good way to make sure that your writing is clear is to let someone else read your paper and make suggestions. Other people may notice things that you have missed.

After you have checked your work, it is helpful to have a peer check it, too. A peer is someone who is equal to you. In this class, your classmates are your peers. When a peer edits your writing, it is called **peer editing**.

This is what usually happens in peer editing:

1. A peer reads your writing.

2. Your peer gives you suggestions and ideas for making your writing better.

3. You listen carefully to what your peer says.

4. You think about making the changes your peer suggests. If the comments are negative, remember that the comments are about the mistakes in your writing, not about you!

There are peer editing sheets that will help you give a classmate good advice about his / her writing on NGL.Cengage.com/GW1. There is a sample in Appendix 3.

ACTIVITY 24 Editing: Grammar and Sentence Review

Correct the paragraph. There are 10 mistakes. The first mistake has been corrected for you.

5 missing *be* verbs   2 capitalization mistakes
2 missing subjects   1 punctuation mistake

The Beauty of Tuscany

Tuscany *is* a beautiful region in Italy. Is famous for cities such as florence, Siena, and Pisa. The amazing apennine Hills in Tuscany. Tuscany *is* also famous for the production of beautiful ceramics. For example, bowls, vases, and oil jars *are* very popular with tourists. Tuscany has so many interesting places to see. Assisi and Siena *are* two beautiful cities that many people love to visit. *It* Is a wonderful place to visit.

Writer's Note

Writing Helpful and Polite Peer Editing Comments

When you peer edit a classmate's writing, choose your words carefully. Make sure that:

- Your comments are helpful. Be specific about the mistakes.

    Not helpful: "This is incorrect."

    Helpful: "You forgot to put the word *at* here."

- Your comments are polite. Say things the way you would want someone to tell you!

    Not polite: "What is this?? It doesn't make any sense at all!"

    Polite: "What does this sentence mean? Can you make the meaning clearer?"

Before you write a comment, ask yourself, "Will this be helpful to the writer? Or will it just make the writer feel bad?" Make sure your comments are helpful <u>and</u> polite.

ACTIVITY 25 **Editing: Practice with Peer Editing Comments**

Look at the paragraph you edited in Activity 24. Imagine that you must give feedback to the writer. Complete the feedback below. (Remember to keep your comments polite and helpful.) Then compare your comments with a classmate.

1. Write one positive comment on the paragraph.

   _____

2. Write one thing the writer can improve when he or she rewrites the paragraph.

   _____

ACTIVITY 26 **Peer Editing**

Exchange books with a partner and look at Activity 22. Read your partner's sentences. Then use Peer Editing Sheet 1 on NGL.Cengage.com/GW1 to help you comment on your partner's sentences. There is a sample in the Appendix. Be sure to offer positive suggestions and comments that will help your partner improve his or her writing. Consider your partner's comments as you revise your own sentences.

Journal Writing

To improve your writing, it is important to write as <u>much</u> as you can and as <u>often</u> as you can.

The Benefit of Practice

Think about people who play a sport like tennis well. They have to <u>practice</u>. It does not matter if they hit the ball the wrong way at first. The most important thing is to hit the ball again and again. This is how people get better at tennis.

In some ways, you are like a tennis player. You want to be a good writer. Reading books about how to write will help you, but one of the best ways to become a good writer in English is to write, write, and write!

Practice in a Journal

An excellent way to practice is to write in a **journal.** A journal is a notebook in which you write things regularly.

In a journal:

- You choose a specific topic and write about it.

- You write to express your ideas about the topic so that readers can understand what you mean.

- The topics can be general or specific. Some examples are:

    General Topics: sports, swimming, food, books, travel, fashion, music

    Specific Topics: my favorite sport, why I am a vegetarian, my first airplane trip

- You write more about your thoughts and feelings than about facts and "correct" information. For example, if you write about a city, do not take information from a book. Instead, write about why you want to visit that city or about the first time you visited it.

- You often use informal language.

Teacher Response

Your teacher will read your journal from time to time. Here is how a journal usually works:

- You write about a topic in your journal. Your teacher reads your writing.

- Your teacher may write some comments in your journal. The communication is like a conversation between the writer (you) and the reader (your teacher).

- Your teacher might make one or two comments about the language, especially if you repeat the same mistake. However, your teacher will not mark all of the mistakes.

- If you have any questions, you can ask your teacher in your journal. For example, if you want to know if you used a grammar point or a vocabulary word correctly, you can write a question in your journal.

Sample Journal

March 21

Sometimes I feel lonely here. My parents are far away, but my
brother is here. His name is Jacob. He is two years older than I am.
He wants to study business administration. He looks like my father.
He is 22 years old.

Before we came here, Jacob and I went to New York City.
We visited some cousins there. Hotels in New York expensive.
We stayed with our cousins. That saved us a lot of money.

I do not my cousins very often, so I was happy. Sometimes
I feel bad because I do not know them very well.

> student writing

This is interesting information. I didn't know that your brother
lives here, too. Do you live together? I've been to New York City,
too, and I know that hotels are VERY expensive there.

Grammar: I circled two places where you forgot to put a verb.
Can you think of some verbs for those sentences?

It was easy to understand the message of your writing here.
Keep up the good work!

> teacher comments

Additional Topics for Writing

Here are ten ideas for journal writing. Choose one or more of them to write about. Follow your teacher's directions. (We recommend that you skip a line after each line that you write. This gives your teacher a place to write comments.)

PHOTO
TOPIC: Look at the photo on pages 2–3. Describe an amazing place in your country. Explain why this place is so unusual and important to you.

TOPIC 2: Write about your mother or your father. Include his/her name, age, and occupation. What kind of personality does your mother or father have?

TOPIC 3: Write about your favorite pet. Why do you like this animal? Do you have one at home? What does the animal look like? What is its name? How old is it?

TOPIC 4: Write about your favorite type of weather. Why do you like this weather? What kind of activities do you do in this weather?

TOPIC 5: Write about a gadget that you have. What kind of gadget is it? What does it do? Why is it helpful?

TOPIC 6: Write about your experience learning English. Why are you studying English? How do you feel about English? What is easy for you to understand in English? What are some difficulties you have in English?

TOPIC 7: Write about your favorite type of fashion in clothing. What kind is it? Why do you like it?

TOPIC 8: Write about an "extreme" sport, such as bungee jumping. How do you feel about this sport? Do you want to try this sport? Why or why not? Describe the types of people who enjoy these kinds of sports.

TOPIC 9: Write about your home. How many rooms are in your home? What color is it? How old is it? Do you like it? What is your favorite room?

TOPIC 10: Write about what you do in your free time. Who do you spend the time with? What activities do you do? How long do you spend doing these activities? Are your free-time activities the same during the week and on weekends?

For more practice with the grammar, vocabulary, and writing found in this unit, go to NGL.Cengage.com/GW1.

Answers to questions on page 4: Italian, Chinese, Hungarian, Romanian, and Arabic.

Understanding Paragraph Basics

Professional rock climber Chris Sharma grips a small indentation in Ceues, France.

OBJECTIVES To learn about adjectives
To understand the parts of a paragraph
To study subject and object pronouns
To learn about possessive adjectives

Can you describe an activity or sport that you enjoy?

Grammar for Writing

Using Adjectives

When you write, you can make a sentence much more interesting if you add descriptive words. These descriptive words are called **adjectives**. They describe **nouns**.

- A **noun** is the name of a person, place, thing, or idea.

  student, doctor, city, park, book, pencil, and love

- An **adjective** is a word that describes a noun.

  good, busy, new, crowded, green, heavy, and beautiful

Word Order: Adjective + Noun

Good writers avoid writing too many simple sentences about one subject. When you have two short sentences about the same noun with an adjective, you can combine the sentences by putting the adjective <u>before</u> the noun. This will make your writing more interesting.

Two Short Sentences	Better Writing
noun adj. I have a **book**. It is <u>heavy</u>.	adj. noun I have a <u>heavy</u> **book**.
noun adj. This is my **car**. It is <u>new</u>.	adj. noun This is my <u>new</u> **car**.
noun adj. Marco goes to a **college**. The college is <u>excellent</u>.	adj. noun Marco goes to an <u>excellent</u> **college**.
adj. noun adj. noun Rachel draws <u>small</u> **pictures**. She draws <u>ink</u> **pictures**.	adj. adj. noun Rachel draws <u>small</u> <u>ink</u> **pictures**.

IMPORTANT: Make sure you put the adjective <u>before</u> the noun, not after.

- ✗ I have a <u>car red</u> with a <u>top black</u>.

- ✓ I have a red car with a black top.

- ✗ We ate a <u>salad green</u> with <u>potatoes fried</u>.

- ✓ We ate a green salad with fried potatoes.

IMPORTANT: Adjectives do not have a plural form to describe plural nouns.

- ✗ There are <u>rares</u> books in the library.

- ✓ There are rare books in the library.

- ✗ Do you like <u>populars</u> songs?

- ✓ Do you like popular songs?

There is more information about order of adjectives on page 239 in the *Brief Writer's Handbook*.

Combine the related sentences into one sentence. You will have to eliminate a few words. Remember to use a capital letter at the beginning and a period at the end of each sentence.

1. Rob owns a car. The car is red.

   Rob owns a red car.

2. I do not like this weather. The weather is humid.

   I do not like the humid weather

3. Paris is a city in France. This city is beautiful.

   Paris is a beautiful city

4. Ali has a job. The job is part-time.

   Ali has a Part-time Job.

5. They like to drink soda. The soda is diet.

   They like to drink diet soda

6. Nina reads folk tales. They are international.

   Nina reads international folk tales

7. My mother grows roses. The roses are big. The roses are beautiful.

   My mother grows roses big and beautiful.

8. Juan works for a company. The company is small. The company is independent.

   Juan works in independent and small company

9. My grandparents live in a town. It is a farming town. The town is small.

   My grandparents live in a small farming town.

10. Sharon rents a house on Smith Street. The house is white. The house is tiny.

    Sharon rents a white, tiny house

Grammar for Writing

Word Order: *Be* + Adjective

If the main verb of a sentence is *be*, the adjective can come <u>after</u> the verb.

Subject	*Be*	Adjective(s)
The boys	are	young.
I	am	sleepy.
That house	is	big and green.

Word Order: Linking Verb + Adjective

The verb *be* is a **linking verb**. A linking verb connects the subject to the adjective that comes after it. These verbs are often (but not always) related to your five natural senses: sight, taste, touch, smell, and hearing.

If the main verb of a sentence is a linking verb, the adjective can come <u>after</u> the verb.

Subject	Linking Verb		Adjective	
Justin	looks		ill.	
The grapes	taste		delicious.	
The hot water	feels		good	on my feet.
These flowers	smell	really	sweet.	
Sohee's plan	sounds		interesting.	
Tony and Ron	seem	very	nervous	today.

Many linking verbs can also be actions verbs. When a linking verb is followed by an adjective, it does not have any action.

Action Verb	My mother	tastes	her soup.
Linking Verb (no action)	The soup	tastes	good.

Underline the 11 adjectives in the paragraph. (The numbers in parentheses on the left side of the paragraph tell you how many adjectives are in each line.) Then circle the linking verbs. The first adjective has been underlined for you.

Example Paragraph 6

My Ideal Vacation

(1) I have a dream to visit Alaska. The weather is <u>beautiful</u> there. I love

(2) cold weather. When the temperature is low, I have energy! I also want

(2) to visit Alaska because I love nature. Alaska looks so **pure** and natural.

(2) I dream about its **scenic** landscape. In addition, there are wild animals.

(2) Finally, I want to learn important information about the **native** people

(1) of Alaska. Their culture sounds very interesting to me. I hope to visit

(1) this wonderful state soon.

pure: clean; not polluted

scenic: having a beautiful natural landscape

native: born in or originally coming from a certain place or country

ACTIVITY 3 Describing a Scene with Adjectives

Write seven to ten sentences about the market in the photo. Write some sentences using **adjective +
noun** and **linking verb + adjective**. Try to write a sentence that includes both forms.

1. The market seems busy.

2. It's a crowded place.

3. Their clothing is colorful.

4. The place is crowded.

5. _____

6. _____

7. _____

8. _____

9. _____

10. _____

What Is a Paragraph?

A **paragraph** is a group of sentences about one specific topic. A paragraph has three main parts: the topic sentence, the body, and the concluding sentence.

ACTIVITY 4 **Studying Paragraphs**

Read each paragraph and answer the questions that follow.

The Best Place to Relax

My back **porch** is my favorite place to **relax**. First, it has lots of comfortable chairs with soft pillows. I feel so good when I sit in them. My back porch is also very peaceful. I can sit and think there. I can even read a great book and nobody **bothers** me. Finally, in the evening, I can sit on my porch and watch the sunset. Watching the beautiful colors always calms me. I can relax in many places, but my back porch is the best.

a porch: a part at the front or back of a house with only a floor and a roof

to relax: to rest or do something enjoyable

to bother: to make someone feel worried or upset

Post-Reading

1. How many sentences are in this paragraph? _____

2. What is the main topic of this paragraph? (Circle.)

   a. The writer likes watching the sunset.

   b. The writer likes to read a book in a quiet place.

   c. The writer likes to relax on her back porch.

3. What is the first sentence of this paragraph? (This is the topic sentence.) Write it here.

   _____

   _____

4. The writer gives examples of how her porch is relaxing. List the four things the writer does to relax on her porch.

   a. ___The writer sits in comfortable chairs._____

   b. _____

   c. _____

   d. _____

5. Read the paragraph again. Find at least two adjectives and write them below.

   _____

6. Read the topic (first) sentence and the concluding (last) sentence of the paragraph. Write down the ideas that these two sentences have in common.

   _____

Example Paragraph 8

Taipei 101

I work in one of the world's tallest buildings—Taipei 101. This building is in Taipei's business **district**. Taipei 101 opened to the public in 2004. It is made of **steel** and glass panels, so it has a beautiful silver color. It has 101 **floors**. There are even five more levels below the building! Many international businesses have offices in Taipei 101. There are great places to shop in the building, too. I am **proud** to work in such an important place.

a district: an area

steel: a very strong metal

a floor: a level of a building

proud: having a very happy feeling of satisfaction

Post-Reading

1. How many sentences are in this paragraph? _____

2. What is the main topic of this paragraph? (Circle.)

   a. information about a city

   b. information about a person

   c. information about a building

3. What is the first sentence of this paragraph? (This is the topic sentence.) Write it here.

   _____

   _____

4. Answer these questions in complete sentences.

   a. Where is the building?

   _____

   b. How old is the building?

   _____

   c. What color is the building?

   _____

   d. How many floors does the building have in total?

   _____

5. Read the paragraph again. Find at least four adjectives and write them below.

   _____

6. Read the topic (first) sentence and the concluding (last) sentence of the paragraph. Write down the ideas that these two sentences have in common.

   _____

The Title of a Paragraph

What is the title of this textbook? Look on the front cover. Write the title here.

_____

What is the title of Example Paragraph 6 on page 37? Write the title here.

_____

A **title** gives the reader information about what is in a book, magazine, song, movie, or paragraph. Here are some rules to follow when you write a title for your paragraphs.

Rule #1: A good title is usually short. Sometimes it is only one word. *Titanic* and *Help* are titles.

Rule #2: A good title is usually <u>not</u> a complete sentence. Some examples of paragraph titles in this book are *Staying Healthy, A World Traveler,* and *An Old Family Photo.*

Rule #3: A good title catches a reader's interest. It tells the reader about the main topic, but it does not tell about everything in the paragraph. *A Long Flight, An Important Invention,* and *My First Car* are all titles of paragraphs in this book. Each one gives you a good idea of what the paragraph will be about. However, it does not give you all the information.

Rule #4: A good title also follows special capitalization rules. Always capitalize the first letter of the first word. Only capitalize the first letter of the important words in the title. Do not capitalize a preposition or an article unless it is the first word.

Rule #5: A title never has a period at the end.

ACTIVITY 5   Working with Titles

Each of these titles breaks at least one of the rules listed on page 42. Rewrite each one correctly. Be prepared to share your answers with your classmates and explain which rule (or rules) the incorrect title breaks.

1. RAP MUSIC AROUND THE WORLD

   _____

2. A Handbook For International Students In Canada

   _____

3. Great Jobs for Teenagers.

   _____

4. My Paragraph

   _____

5. How to Upload Your Family Vacation Photos to the Internet

   _____

6. Buying A New Car Is Easy

   _____

7. The ten Best Movies of All Time

   _____

8. Today Was the Best day of My Life

   _____

Writer's Note

Indenting the First Line of Every Paragraph

Look at the first line of Example Paragraph 7 on page 39. How is the formatting different from the other lines in the paragraph?

Look at the first line of Example Paragraph 8 on page 40. Do you see how the first line is also moved in? This is called **indenting**. It is important to **indent** the first line of every paragraph because it tells the reader that a new paragraph is beginning.

ACTIVITY 6 Copying a Paragraph

On the lines below, copy the six sentences about ice cream from Activity 13 on page 16 (Unit 1). Be sure to indent the first line. Use correct punctuation at the end of each sentence. Give this paragraph a title. When you finish, read your new paragraph.

Example Paragraph 9 _____

_____

_____

_____

_____

_____

_____

_____

_____

_____

_____

_____

_____

_____

ACTIVITY 7 Writing an Original Paragraph

Answer the questions. Use complete sentences. Then write your sentences in paragraph form on the lines provided.

1. Who is your favorite singer? __My favorite singer is__ _____

2. What country does he or she come from? _____

3. What kind of music does he or she sing? _____

    _____

4. What is your favorite song by this singer? _____

    _____

5. Why do you like this singer? _____

    _____

Now write your sentences in paragraph form. Be sure to indent the first line. Give your paragraph a title.

_____

_____

_____

_____

_____

_____

_____

_____

_____

_____

_____

Parts of a Paragraph: The Topic Sentence

Every good paragraph has a **topic sentence**. The topic sentence is one sentence that tells the main idea of the whole paragraph.

The topic sentence:

- is usually the first sentence in the paragraph
- should not be too specific or too general
- must describe the information in all the sentences of the paragraph

If a paragraph does not have a topic sentence, the reader may be confused because the ideas will not be organized clearly. Make sure every paragraph has a topic sentence!

Practicing Topic Sentences

Read each paragraph and the three topic sentences below it. Choose the best topic sentence and write it on the lines. Then read the paragraph again. Make sure that the topic sentence gives the main idea for the whole paragraph. Remember to indent.

Example Paragraph 11

Beautiful Snow?

_____ Snow is beautiful when it falls. After a few days, the snow is not beautiful anymore. It starts to **melt**, and the clean streets become **messy**. It is difficult to walk anywhere. The **sidewalks** are **slippery**. Snow also causes traffic problems. Some roads are closed. Other roads are **hard** to drive on safely. Drivers have more **accidents** on snowy roads. I understand why some people like snow, but I do not like it very much.

   a. In December, it usually snows.

   b. Some people like snow, but I do not.

   c. I love snow.

to melt: to change from ice to liquid

messy: sloppy; dirty

a sidewalk: a paved walkway on the side of roads

slippery: causing a person to slip or slide, usually because of a smooth surface

hard: difficult

an accident: a car crash

Maria and Her Great Job

_____ She works at Papa Joe's Restaurant. She **serves** about 60 people every day. Maria can remember all the dinner orders. If there is a problem with any of the food, she **takes** it **back** to the kitchen **immediately.** Maria works very hard to make sure all her customers have a great meal.

    a. My cousin Maria is an excellent server.

    b. My cousin Maria works at Papa Joe's Restaurant.

    c. Maria's customers do not eat big meals.

to serve: to give someone food and drink at a restaurant

to take back: to return

immediately: at that moment; very quickly

My Favorite City

_____ I love to see all the interesting things there. The city is big, exciting, and full of life. I always visit the Statue of Liberty and the Empire State Building. I also visit Chinatown. At night, I go to **shows** on Broadway. The food in the city is excellent, too. I truly enjoy New York City.

    a. I like to see the Statue of Liberty and the Empire State Building.

    b. New York is a very big city.

    c. My favorite city in the world is New York.

a show: a live performance on stage

Read each paragraph on pages 48–50 and the four topic sentences below it. Choose the best topic sentence and write it on the lines. Then read the paragraph again. Make sure that the topic sentence gives the main idea for the whole paragraph. Be sure to indent! (NOTE: If you want a challenge, cover the four topic sentences, and try to write your own. Is your topic sentence similar to the correct topic sentence?)

Example Paragraph 14

Pasta, Pasta, Pasta

_____

_____ Pasta tastes great. Sometimes I eat it **plain**. I also like it with butter or **Parmesan cheese**. Another reason I like pasta is the **variety**. Pasta includes spaghetti, macaroni, vermicelli, ravioli, lasagna, and many other kinds. In addition, pasta is very easy to prepare. I can make pasta in less than ten minutes. Finally, pasta is a very healthy food for me. A plate of pasta has about 300 **calories**, but it has only three grams of fat. I love to eat pasta every day!

a. Everybody loves pasta.

b. Spaghetti and macaroni are kinds of pasta.

c. Pasta is my favorite food.

d. Pasta comes from Italy.

plain: with nothing added; simple

Parmesan cheese: a hard, dry Italian cheese

a variety: many different kinds

a calorie: a measurement of heat energy of food

Good Teachers

_____

_____ First of all, good teachers
are **patient**. They never **rush** their students. Good teachers explain
things without getting **bored**. In addition, they are organized. They
plan what happens in every class. Good teachers are also **encouraging**.
They help students understand the subject. Finally, good teachers are **fair**.
They treat all students the same. These are some of the most important
qualities of good teachers.

    a. All good teachers are patient.

    b. Good teachers have special qualities.

    c. I like my teachers.

    d. Some teachers are good, but other teachers are not so good.

patient: calm; not easily upset

to rush: to cause (someone or something) to go very quickly

bored: not interested

encouraging: helpful; comforting

fair: equal; impartial

Awesome Internet Radio

_____

_____ First, I can listen to radio stations from around the world, so I have a variety of musical choices. I can choose bhangra from a New Delhi station or the newest music from a station in England. I can also listen to individual music stations that people create. I follow several popular **disc jockeys** in Los Angeles and New York. I also like Internet radio's **convenience**. I do not need to stay at home or use my car to listen to the radio. I can listen on my smartphone and my mp3 player **whenever** and **wherever** I want. However, the best thing of all is that Internet radio is free! I cannot imagine music without Internet radio!

a disc jockey: a radio announcer who plays music

convenience: an increase in comfort or easiness in work

whenever: at any time

wherever: in any place

    a. Before the Internet, people only listened to the radio one way.

    b. There are great radio stations all over the world.

    c. People all over the world like listening to the radio.

    d. Internet radio is the perfect way for me to listen to music.

Grammar for Writing

Subject Pronouns

A **pronoun** is a word that takes the place of a noun. A **subject pronoun** is a pronoun that takes the place of a noun that is the <u>subject</u> in a sentence.

Subject Pronoun (Singular)		Subject Pronoun (Plural)	
I	live in Panama.	We	live in Panama.
You	work in a bank.	You	work in a bank.
He / She / It	is from Turkey.	They	are from Turkey.

Object Pronouns

An **object pronoun** is a pronoun that takes the place of a noun that is the <u>object</u> in a sentence.

	Object Pronoun (Singular)		Object Pronoun (Plural)
Mona likes	**me.**	Mona likes	**us.**
I know	**you.**	I know	**you.**
Kevin understands	**him / her / it.**	Kevin understands	**them.**

An object pronoun can also replace the noun after a **preposition**. A preposition is a word that shows location, time, or direction. Some common prepositions are *in, on, to,* and *near.*

	Preposition	Object Pronoun
Assad walks	**with**	me.
They give help	**to**	us. you.
Jessica lives	**near**	him / her / it. them.

ACTIVITY 10 **Using Subject Pronouns**

Replace the noun(s) in parentheses with a subject pronoun.

Example Paragraph 17

Two Doctors

Rosemarie Bertrand and Michael Scott are interesting people. Rosemarie is a doctor in Scotland. (**1.** Rosemarie Bertrand) _____She_____ is married to Michael. (**2.** Michael Scott) _____ is also a doctor. (**3.** Rosemarie and Michael) _____ live in Edinburgh. (**4.** Edinburgh) _____ is a historic city. Dr. Bertrand and Dr. Scott have an office together downtown. (**5.** The office) _____ is busy every day. (**6.** Rosemarie and Michael) _____ work hard five days a week. On weekends, however, (**7.** Rosemarie and Michael) _____ like to travel to the countryside. (**8.** The countryside) _____ is a beautiful and relaxing escape from all their hard work.

ACTIVITY 11 Using Object Pronouns

Replace the noun(s) in parentheses with an object pronoun.

Example Paragraph 18

My Best Friend

My best friend is Gretchen. I met (**1.** Gretchen) _____*her*_____

ten years ago. She is from Alabama. She comes from a very large family.

She has four brothers and three sisters. She does not live with (**2.** her

brothers and sisters) _____ . They live in Alabama with their

parents. Gretchen studies **veterinary** medicine at the University of

Florida in Gainesville. She loves (**3.** her career choice) _____

very much because she really loves animals. Gretchen has three pets.

She has a cat, a small bird, and a large boa constrictor, Hal. She likes (**4.**

her pets) _____ all very much. However, she likes Hal the best.

Gretchen takes (**5.** Hal) _____ with (**6.** Gretchen) _____

everywhere! In her free time, Gretchen plays tennis, reads books,

and cooks **gourmet** meals. I love (**7.** Gretchen) _____ like a

sister. I hope that our friendship will stay with (**8.** Gretchen and me)

_____ for many years.

veterinary: medical
care of animals

gourmet: producing
extremely good food
and drink

Using Pronouns to Make Your Writing More Interesting

When you write about a noun, using the same noun again and again in your paragraph can make your writing sound repetitive.

> **Alisa** lives in the city. **Alisa** likes the noise and the crowds, but **Alisa** does not like the stress.
> Kris has **a new car**. He washes **his new car** every day. **His new car** is fun, and **his new car** is fast!

To make your writing more interesting, replace some nouns with pronouns.

> **Alisa** lives in the city. **She** likes the noise and the crowds, but **she** does not like the stress.
> Kris has **a new car**. He washes **it** every day. **His new car** is fun, and **it** is fast!

ACTIVITY 12 Using Subject and Object Pronouns for Variety

This paragraph uses the same nouns too many times. Cross out some nouns, and replace them with subject or object pronouns.

Example Paragraph 19

Our Big Move

Amy and I are moving into our new apartment today. ~~Amy and I~~ *We* are very excited. Amy and I have many big things to put in our new apartment. I have a large flat screen TV. Amy and I plan to put the television next to the window. Amy's brother and his friends will help Amy and I move today, too. Amy's brother and his friends will move our large **couch** and chairs. Amy and I want to put the couch and chairs in front of the television. Finally, Amy's brother and his friends will move in our beds. It may take a long time to move the beds because the beds are so big. However, Amy and I are not worried because our strong helpers will make the move easy!

a couch: a piece of furniture big enough for three or more people to sit on

Parts of a Paragraph: The Body

Every good paragraph must have sentences that support the topic sentence. These supporting sentences are called the **body** of a paragraph.

The supporting sentences:

- give more information, such as **support, details**, or **examples**, about the topic sentence
- must be related to the topic sentence
- should <u>not</u> include ideas that are unrelated or unconnected to the topic sentence

A good body can make your paragraph stronger, so make sure EVERY sentence in your body is related to the topic sentence.

One mistake that many writers make is writing sentences that are not related to the topic sentence. Be sure to cut out any unrelated or unconnected ideas.

Fill in each blank with the correct possessive adjective.

Example Paragraph 23

Kate and Her Siblings

Kate has two sisters and one brother. **1** _____Their_____ names
are Ashley, Julia, and Nick. Ashley and Julia live with **2** _____
parents. They are high school students. Ashley likes to play sports.
3 _____ favorite sport is softball. She is a very good player.
Julia does not like sports, but she loves music. She plays
4 _____ guitar every afternoon after school. Ashley and Julia
have the same friends. **5** _____ friends go to the same school.
6 _____ brother, Nick, is in college. **7** _____ major
is business administration. Kate's brother and sisters are all very different,
but she loves **8** _____ **siblings** very much.

> **a sibling:** a brother or a sister

ACTIVITY 15 Practicing Subject Pronouns and Possessive Adjectives

Underline the correct pronoun or possessive adjective.

Example Paragraph 24

(I / <u>My</u>) Grandmother

A very important person in (**1.** I / my) life is (**2.** I / my)
grandmother. (**3.** She / Her) name is Evelyn Anna Kratz. (**4.** She / Her)
life is very interesting. (**5.** She / Her) is 89 years old. (**6.** She / Her) comes
from Poland. (**7.** She / Her) can speak English well, but (**8.** she / her)
first language is Polish. My grandmother comes from a large family.
(**9.** She / Her) has two brothers. (**10.** They / Their) names are Peter and
John. (**11.** I / My) grandmother has two sisters, too. (**12.** They / Their)
names are Karina and Maria. (**13.** I / My) like to listen to (**14.** my / her)
grandmother's stories because (**15.** they / their) are so interesting. In (**16.**
I / my) opinion, they are the most interesting stories in the world.

Working with the Body of a Paragraph

Read each paragraph carefully. In each paragraph, there are two sentences that do not belong. Put parentheses ( ) around the two unrelated sentences.

Example Paragraph 25

The *New* States

Four U.S. states begin with the word *new*. New Hampshire, New Jersey, and New York are in the Northeast, but New Mexico is in the Southwest. Arizona is also in the Southwest. New Hampshire is a small state with just over one million people. New Jersey is also a small state, but its population is almost nine million people. The most **well-known** of the *new* states is New York. With twenty million people, its population is the largest of all the *new* states. Finally, there is New Mexico. It is the largest in size of these four states, but its population is really quite small with a little over two million people. There are no states that begin with the word *old*. Although all these states begin with new, they are all very different.

well-known: popular, familiar, famous

An Incredible Neighbor

My neighbor Mrs. Wills is an **amazing** person. She is 96 years old. My grandmother lived to be 87. Mrs. Wills lives alone, and she takes care of herself. In the morning, she works in her beautiful garden. She also does all of her own cooking. She does not like to cook rice. She cleans her own house. She even puts her heavy garbage can by the street for trash collection. She pulls it slowly to the **curb**, and she goes up and down the steps to her door without help. I hope to have that much energy and ability when I am 96 years old.

amazing: remarkable; wonderful; incredible

the curb: the side of the street

My Office

My office has everything I need to do my work. On the left side of the room, there is a big **wooden** desk. My computer sits on top of the desk, and the printer sits under it. I keep paper **files** in its drawers. On the right side of the room, there are two beautiful bookcases. My father makes bookcases and other wood furniture. They are full of books, magazines, and computer software. There is also a telephone and a fax machine on a small table next to my closet. I have trouble remembering my fax number. All my office supplies are in it. I enjoy my office very much.

wooden: made of wood

files: documents; papers

ACTIVITY 17 **Review: Identifying Subject and Object Pronouns and Possessive Adjectives**

Look at the paragraphs in Activity 16 again. Circle all the subject pronouns. Underline all the possessive adjectives. Put a box around the object pronouns. Check your answers with a classmate.

Writer's Note

Avoiding Fragments: Checking for the Verb

As you write, remember that every sentence needs a verb. A sentence without a verb is a fragment. It is a piece of a sentence, not a complete sentence.

✗ My father's name Samuel.

✗ Many people in Switzerland French.

✗ Some elementary schools computers for the students.

✓ My father's name is Samuel.

✓ Many people in Switzerland speak French.

✓ Some elementary schools have computers for the students.

ACTIVITY 18   Editing: Checking for Verbs

Five sentences below are missing the verb *be*. Add the correct form of *be* to the incomplete sentences. Then put the sentences in the correct order. The first missing *be* verb has been corrected for you.

Staying Healthy

_____ **a.** Doctors say that one hour of exercise each day can keep you in good shape.

_____ **b.** First, think about the food you eat.

__1__ **c.** It *is* easy to stay healthy if you **follow** some simple **steps**.

_____ **d.** This allows your body to rest and become stronger.

_____ **e.** You can follow these steps to help yourself stay healthy.

_____ **f.** The best **types** of food fruits and vegetables.

_____ **g.** In addition, exercise good for your mind and emotions.

_____ **h.** Finally, relaxation very important.

_____ **i.** It important to eat a lot of them every day.

_____ **j.** Next, **consider** some exercise.

to follow: to obey, do

steps: directions

a type: a kind

to consider: to think about

59

Turn back to Activity 9 on page 12 in Unit 1. Check your sentences for missing verbs. Rewrite three of your sentences with missing verbs correctly on the lines below (even if your teacher already corrected your work). If you did not make any mistakes, good job! Use the lines below to write about a new topic using the same format as Activity 9.

_____

_____

_____

_____

_____

_____

_____

_____

Parts of a Paragraph: The Concluding Sentence

In addition to a topic sentence and body, every good paragraph has a **concluding sentence**. The concluding sentence ends the paragraph with a final thought.

The concluding sentence:

- often gives a summary of the information in the paragraph
- often gives information that is similar to the information in the topic sentence
- can be a **suggestion**, **opinion**, or **prediction**
- should <u>not</u> give any new information about the topic

Look at the topic sentences and concluding sentences from a few paragraphs in this unit.

	Paragraph 6, Page 37	**Paragraph 7, Page 39**	**Paragraph 8, Page 40**
Topic Sentence	I have a dream to visit Alaska.	My back porch is my favorite place to relax.	I work in one of the world's tallest buildings—Taipei 101.
Concluding Sentence	I hope to visit this wonderful state soon.	I can relax in many places, but my back porch is the best.	I am proud to work in such an important place.

ACTIVITY 20 Working with Concluding Sentences

Copy the topic sentence and concluding sentence from each paragraph indicated. How are the two sentences the same? How are they different? Discuss your answers with a partner.

1. Example Paragraph 11, page 46

   Topic sentence: _____

   Concluding sentence: _____

   _____

2. Example Paragraph 12, page 47

   Topic sentence: _____

   Concluding sentence: _____

   _____

3. Example Paragraph 13, page 47

   Topic sentence: _____

   Concluding sentence: _____

4. Example Paragraph 14, page 48

   Topic sentence: _____

   Concluding sentence: _____

5. Example Paragraph 15, page 49

   Topic sentence: _____

   Concluding sentence: _____

   _____

6. Example Paragraph 16, page 50

   Topic sentence: _____

   Concluding sentence: _____

ACTIVITY 21 Choosing Concluding Sentences

Read each paragraph and the three concluding sentences below it. Choose the best concluding sentence and write it on the lines. Then read the paragraph again. Make sure that the concluding sentence gives a final thought for the whole paragraph.

Example Paragraph 28

Monday

I hate Monday for many reasons. One reason is work. I get up early to go to work on Monday. After a weekend of fun and relaxation, I do not like to do this. Another reason that I do not like Monday is that I have three meetings every Monday. These meetings last a long time, and they are **extremely** boring. Traffic is also a big problem on Monday. There are more cars on the road on Monday. Drivers are in a bad **mood**, and I must be more careful than usual. _____

_____

extremely: very

a mood: a person's emotion at a particular time

    a. Monday is worse than Tuesday, but it is better than Sunday.

    b. I do not like meetings on Monday.

    c. These are just a few reasons why I do not like Monday.

Example Paragraph 29

Buying a Car

Buying a car **requires** careful planning. Do you want a new or a used car? This depends on how much money you can spend. Sometimes a used car needs repairs. What style of car do you want? You can look at many different models to help you decide. Next, do you want extra **features** in your new car? Adding lots of extra features makes a car more expensive. Finally, you have to decide where you will buy your car. _____

_____

to require: to need

a feature: an option, such as a DVD player or tinted windows

    a. It is important to think about all of these things when you are buying a car.

    b. The most important thing is the kind of car that you want to buy.

    c. Will you buy your new car from a friend or a car dealer?

Hanami

Hanami is a very popular Japanese tradition. Every spring, thousands of **cherry** trees bloom all over Japan. For two weeks during Hanami, friends and families gather in parks and the countryside to see the beautiful flowers and celebrate the end of their vacation time. People make lots of food and have huge picnics under the lovely trees. There is lots of music and dancing, and large groups of people walk through the parks together. The celebration often continues into the night, and there are **lanterns** everywhere to light the celebration. _____

_____

a cherry: a small red fruit

a lantern: a light with a decorative cover

    a. People like to be with their family and friends during Hanami.

    b. Looking at flowers during Hanami is interesting.

    c. This is truly a most beloved Japanese custom.

Editing: Grammar and Sentence Review

Correct the paragraph. There are 7 mistakes.

3 adjective mistakes   2 missing *be* verbs
2 capitalization mistakes

Example Paragraph 31

Aspirin

aspirin is an incredible type of medicine. This small white pill is not a drug new. We do not know exactly why or how it works. However, millions of people use aspirin every day. We take aspirin for reasons many. Aspirin good for headaches, colds, and pain. Aspirin can help with so many different Health problems. Aspirin is a medicine simple, but it great.

Building Better Sentences: For further practice with the sentences and paragraphs in this unit, go to Practice 2 on page 254 in Appendix 1.

Building Better Vocabulary

Word Associations

Circle the word or phrase that is most closely related to the word or phrase on the left. If necessary, use a dictionary to check the meaning of words you do not know.

	A	B
1. an opinion	a belief	a fact
2. a headache	pain	relaxation
3. to consider	to talk to	to think about
4. to spend	money comes in	money goes out
5. historic	career	city
6. furniture	a rug	a sofa

7. to come from	a destination	an origin
8. afternoon	darkness	daylight
9. to serve	to give	to take
10. traffic	pedestrians	vehicles
11. downtown	a city center	a suburb
12. to prepare	food	a headache
13. to organize	to make messy	to make neat
14. a variety	few choices	many choices

ACTIVITY 24 **Using Collocations**

Fill in each blank with the word that most naturally completes the phrase on the right. If necessary, use a dictionary to check the meaning of words you do not know.

1. idea / ideal   an _____ job

2. of / for   a variety _____ ideas

3. do / follow   to _____ a recipe

4. to / for   to prepare _____ an emergency

5. have / make   to _____ an accident

6. be / get   to _____ worth

7. in / on   to major _____ engineering

8. in / on   to be _____ the third floor

9. eat / take   to _____ an aspirin

10. high / tall   a _____ temperature

Study the word forms. Fill in each blank with the best word form provided. Use the correct form of the verb. If necessary, use a dictionary to check the meaning of words you do not know. (NOTE: The word in bold is the original word that appears in the unit.)

Noun	Verb	Adjective	Sentence Practice
dream	**dream**	Ø	1. She _____ about becoming a famous singer.
			2. My _____ is to travel to India.
love	**love**	**lovely**	3. Your dress is _____.
			4. Mario and Yumiko _____ hip-hop music.
problem	Ø	problem**atic**	5. There is a _____ with my car's air conditioning.
			6. The economic situation is _____.
enjoy**ment**	**enjoy**	enjoy**able**	7. The live music is here for everyone's _____.
			8. We always have an _____ time on vacation.
pati**ence**	Ø	**patient**	9. Good teachers have a lot of _____.
			10. My mother is a very _____ woman.

Noun endings: *-ment, -ence*

Adjective endings: *-ly, -atic, -able*

Original Student Writing

Follow these instructions:

- Answer the questions about an interesting person that you know. Use a complete sentence for each answer. Put a check (✓) next to each question as you answer it.

- As you write, use at least two of the vocabulary words or phrases presented in Activity 23, Activity 24, and Activity 25 in your sentences. Underline these words and phrases in your sentences.

- Copy your sentences into a paragraph on the lines provided on page 67.

- Use the checklist on page 68 to edit your work.

_____ 1. Who is the most interesting person you know? _____

_____ 2. How do you know this person?_____

_____ 3. Why is this person interesting? List three reasons why this person is so interesting. Give an example to support each reason. (Use adjectives in your descriptions.)

    a. Reason 1: _____

        Support: _____

    b. Reason 2: _____

        Support: _____

    c. Reason 3: _____

        Support: _____

If you need ideas for words and phrases, see the Useful Vocabulary for Better Writing on pages 247–249.

Example Paragraph 32

_____

_____

_____

_____

_____

_____

_____

_____

_____

_____

_____

_____

_____

_____

_____

_____

☑ Checklist

1. ❏ I used adjectives to describe this person.

2. ❏ I used adjectives before nouns.

3. ❏ I used adjectives after linking verbs.

4. ❏ I indented the first line of my paragraph.

5. ❏ I used subject and object pronouns to add variety.

6. ❏ I used possessive adjectives to show ownership.

7. ❏ I wrote a topic sentence and a concluding sentence. I made sure they are connected in meaning.

8. ❏ I checked each sentence in my paragraph. I made sure every sentence is related to my topic.

9. ❏ I gave my paragraph a title.

ACTIVITY 27 Peer Editing

Exchange books with a partner and look at Activity 26. Read your partner's paragraph. Then use Peer Editing Sheet 2 on NGL.Cengage.com/GW1 to help you comment on your partner's paragraph. Be sure to offer positive suggestions and comments that will help your partner improve his or her writing. Consider your partner's comments as you revise your own paragraph.

Additional Topics for Writing

Here are ten ideas for journal writing. Choose one or more of them to write about. Follow your teacher's directions. (We recommend that you skip a line after each line that you write. This gives your teacher a place to write comments.)

PHOTO
TOPIC: Look at the photo on pages 32–33. Write about an activity or sport that you enjoy. Do you like to practice? How often? Why do you enjoy this activity or sport?

TOPIC 2: Write about an interesting city. What do you know about it? Do you want to visit this city? Why or why not?

TOPIC 3: Write about a good weekend plan. What do you like to do on weekends? Who do you spend your weekends with?

TOPIC 4: Write about how to use an object such as a smartphone or electronic tablet. Explain the steps involved in using this object.

TOPIC 5: Write about credit cards. What is your opinion about them? Are they helpful or dangerous? Do you use them?

TOPIC 6: Write about your favorite kind of music. Why do you like this music? How do you feel when you listen to this music?

TOPIC 7: Choose a person in your class to write about. Explain how the person looks and what his or her personality is like.

TOPIC 8: Write about a famous person you like. Who is this person? What is this person's job? Why do you like this person?

TOPIC 9: Write about something that you do not like. Give three reasons why you do not like this thing. Explain how this thing makes you feel.

TOPIC 10: Write about your favorite subject in school. Why do you like this subject? What kinds of things do you practice in this subject?

For more practice with the grammar, vocabulary, and writing found in this unit, go to NGL.Cengage.com/GW1.

Writing about the Present

Young Rajasthani girls carry water across the desert near Jaisalmer, India.

OBJECTIVES To learn the simple present tense
To study simple and compound sentences
To practice the articles *a* and *an*

*Can you write about things
you do every day?*

Grammar for Writing

The Simple Present Tense: Statements

Use the **simple present tense** to write about:

- daily habits or routines

    Max checks his e-mail each morning.

- general truths

    Children go to school.

    Fish live in water.

Be	
I **am**	we **are**
you **are**	you (plural) **are**
he / she / it **is**	they **are**

Visit / Leave / Carry	
I **visit** leave carry	we **visit** leave carry
you **visit** leave carry	you (plural) **visit** leave carry
he / she / it **visits** leaves carries	they **visit** leave carry

Have	
I **have**	we **have**
you **have**	you (plural) **have**
he / she / it **has**	they **have**

IMPORTANT: Verbs for third person singular subjects (*he, she, it, Nick, Sylvia*) end in **−s** or **−es**.

✗ He call his parents every day.

✓ He calls his parents every day.

✗ I be a student.

✗ I is a student.

✓ I am a student.

✗ He have homework every day.

✓ He has homework every day.

✓ We have homework every day.

Fill in the blanks with the correct simple present tense form of the verb in parentheses.

Uncle Charlie and Aunt Valerie

My Uncle Charlie and Aunt Valerie (**1.** be) _____

successful entrepreneurs. Their restaurant (**2.** be) _____

ten years old now, and they (**3.** enjoy) _____ great success.

The restaurant (**4.** have) _____ 15 servers, two managers,

and three chefs. Uncle Charlie (**5.** work) _____ very

hard in his restaurant. Sometimes he (**6.** be) _____ there

seven days a week. Aunt Valerie always (**7.** go) _____

to the restaurant at night to make sure that the customers (**8.** be)

_____ happy. I (**9.** love) _____ my Uncle

Charlie and Aunt Valerie, and I really appreciate all their hard work.

There (**10.** be) _____ no one better than them!

ACTIVITY 2 Practicing the Simple Present Tense

Fill in the blanks with the correct simple present form of the verbs in the word bank. Some verbs may be used more than once.

love	play	be	speak	come	practice	have

My Classmates

My classmates come from all over the world. José

1 _____ from Spain, so he **2** _____

Spanish perfectly. Wonbin and Hyun-Ju **3** _____

Korean, but they **4** _____ from different cities. Yuri

5 _____ from Ukraine. He **6** _____

English all the time and **7** _____ a great accent. The

Al-Ahmad brothers **8** _____ from Dubai, and they

9 _____ soccer very well. What about me? I

10 _____ from Italy, and I **11** _____ to

sing in class. We **12** _____ all very good friends, and I

hope we can be friends forever.

Number the sentences in the correct paragraph order.

Jim's Daily Routine

_____ **a.** After this part-time job, he goes home, eats a quick dinner, studies, and does his homework.

___2___ **b.** He studies engineering at City College.

_____ **c.** He goes to school for six hours.

_____ **d.** Jim knows that this lifestyle is stressful.

___1___ **e.** Jim is a very busy student.

_____ **f.** Every morning, he wakes up at 7:00, takes a shower, and then rushes off to school.

_____ **g.** He also knows that the stress will end soon, and he will get a professional job.

_____ **h.** After school, he goes to the local mall where he works in a sporting goods store.

ACTIVITY 4 Changing Singular Verbs to Plural Verbs

Make the following changes to the sentences in Activity 3, and rewrite the paragraph in the correct order.

1. Change the subject of the story from _Jim_ to _Jim and Matt_.

2. Make any necessary changes to verb forms, nouns, and pronouns.

Example Paragraph 35

Jim and Matt's Daily Routine

Jim and Matt are very busy students.

_____

_____

_____

_____

_____

_____

_____

_____

_____

_____

Writer's Note

Using Contractions

A contraction is a shortened form of two words combined with an apostrophe (').
The apostrophe takes the place of the missing letter.

I am = I'm

you are = you're

he is = he's / she is = she's / it is = it's

we are = we're

you (plural) are = you're

they are = they're

Contractions are often used in informal writing. Ask your instructor if using contractions
in your academic writing is acceptable in your class.

ACTIVITY 5 Editing: Subjects and Verbs

Correct the paragraph. There are 7 mistakes. The first mistake has been corrected for you.

2 missing subjects   5 missing verbs

Example Paragraph 36

The City of Budapest

Budapest $\overset{is}{\wedge}$ one of the most interesting capitals of Europe. Is a romantic
city, and it has many interesting tourist places to visit. One example the
Danube River. It separates Budapest into Buda and Pest. In addition, visitors
traditional Hungarian food. The most popular food goulash soup. The people
of Budapest friendly and helpful to tourists. When travel to Europe, you can
visit Budapest and have a very good time.

Study the pictures on page 76. They tell a story. Then read the incomplete paragraph. Fill in the blanks based on the pictures. You may need to add two or more words in each blank. Write the full sentence for the last two sentences. NOTE: The numbers in the paragraph correspond to the pictures.

Example Paragraph 37

One Family's Morning Routine

The Lee family is very busy on weekday mornings. **1** Every morning Susan Lee, the oldest daughter, wakes up and _____ for her parents and siblings. She loves to cook in the mornings! **2** When the food is ready, the rest of the family _____ . The kids eat their breakfast quickly. **3** After they eat, Susan's father and mother _____ . **4** At 8:30 A.M., Mr. Lee _____ and sees that it is time to leave. **5** Then he and the kids _____ to Mrs. Lee. **6** Mr. Lee and the kids _____ the minivan so that he can take them to school.

7 _____

8 A few minutes later, _____ .

The Lees certainly do a lot before their work and school day begins!

Grammar for Writing

There Is / There Are

Use **There is** and **There are** to show that something exists in a certain place. Use *is* with singular subjects. Use *are* with plural subjects.

There	*Is / Are*	Subject	(Place Phrase)
There	**is**	a magazine	on the table.
There	**is**	milk	in the refrigerator.
There	**are**	magazines	at the library.
There	**are**	yellow birds.	

✗ There is ten people in my office.
✓ There are ten people in my office.

✗ Is a desk in the room.
✓ There is a desk in the room.

✗ Apples on the table.
✓ There are apples on the table.

✗ A concert at the university tomorrow.
✓ There is a concert at the university tomorrow.

Study the four examples of *there is* and *there are* in the paragraph below. Then answer the questions.

Example Paragraph 38

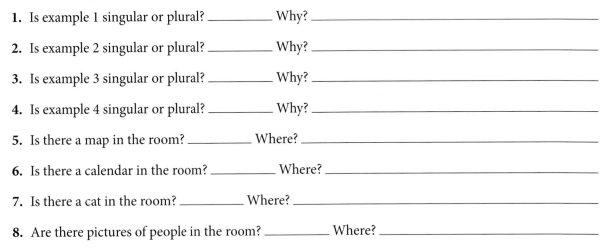

My Colorful Classroom

My classroom is a very colorful room. **1** *There are* twenty desks in the room. Each desk has a dark brown seat and a shiny white top. On the left side of the room, **2** *there is* a world map. This map shows all the different countries in the world, and each country is a different color. On the right side of the room, **3** *there are* two posters. The first poster is green. It has a list of fifty common verbs. The second poster has the names and pictures of fruits and vegetables. It is white, but the writing is black. Finally, **4** *there are* some pictures of famous leaders above the whiteboard. These objects make my classroom colorful.

Post-Reading

1. Is example 1 singular or plural? _____ Why? _____

2. Is example 2 singular or plural? _____ Why? _____

3. Is example 3 singular or plural? _____ Why? _____

4. Is example 4 singular or plural? _____ Why? _____

5. Is there a map in the room? _____ Where? _____

6. Is there a calendar in the room? _____ Where? _____

7. Is there a cat in the room? _____ Where? _____

8. Are there pictures of people in the room? _____ Where? _____

ACTIVITY 8 Using *There Is / There Are*

Write ten sentences about the objects in the picture of the living room. Use *there is* and *there are*. You may use the words in the box to help you. (To see examples of words that begin place phrases, see page 241 in the *Brief Writer's Handbook*.)

bookshelf	picture	television	TV console	couch
pillows	coffee table	chair	rug	vase
bowl	watch	magazines	remote control	books

1. _____

2. _____

3. _____

4. _____

5. _____

6. _____

7. _____

8. _____

9. _____

10. _____

ACTIVITY 9 Editing Practice

The paragraph below has four mistakes with verbs and *There is / There are*. Circle and correct the mistakes. Then explain your corrections.

Example Paragraph 39

The English Alphabet

There have 26 letters in the English alphabet. There is five vowel letters and 21 consonant letters. The five vowels are *a, e, i, o,* and *u.* The letters *w* and *y* can be vowels when they come after other vowels. There three letters with the *a* sound in their names. These letters are *a, j,* and *k.* Are nine letters with the *e* sound in their names. These are *b, c, d, e, g, p, t, v,* and *z.* If you want to speak English well, you have to learn the 26 letters of the English alphabet.

1. _____

2. _____

3. _____

4. _____

Writer's Note

There are vs. They are

Be careful not to confuse *There are* and *They are.*

- **There are** shows that something exists in a particular location. The subject of the sentence comes after *are* (*There are* + subject).

- **They are** is the beginning of a sentence about a group of people or things. The subject of the sentence is *They.*

    ✗ They are five people in my family.

    ✓ There are five people in my family.

    ✗ Piano keys have two colors. There are black and white.

    ✓ Piano keys have two colors. They are black and white.

ACTIVITY 10 Practicing *They Are* vs. *There Are*

Fill in the blanks with *There are* or *They are.*

1. _____ too many questions on this test!

2. _____ happy to see us today.

3. _____ at the doctor.

4. _____ many different ways to study English.

5. _____ some apples in the kitchen.

6. _____ at the store right now.

7. _____ my best friends in the whole world.

8. _____ two servers in the restaurant.

9. _____ great teachers at our school.

10. _____ excited about Mark's party.

ACTIVITY 11 Editing: Capitalization Review

Correct the paragraph. There are 11 capitalization mistakes. The first mistake has been corrected for you.

Example Paragraph 40

Amazing Tourist Towers

Did you know that many popular travel spots are former World's **Fair** towers? The most famous is the Eiffel Ṯower from the 1889 fair in paris. This tall **graceful** tower is a well-known symbol of france. Tourists often ride boats on the Seine river at night and look at the tower's beautiful lights. Another famous fair tower is in seattle,

a fair: an outdoor entertainment event with rides, games, and displays

graceful: moving in a smooth and beautiful way

Washington, in the united States. The space Needle comes from the 1962 World's Fair, and it looks like a giant tower with a **UFO** on top of it. people love to eat in the **revolving** restaurant at the top. In Daejeon, South korea, travelers love to visit the Tower of grand Light from the 1993 World's Fair. This silver and red tower is now part of a giant amusement park where people can swim, watch movies, and enjoy exciting rides. These are only a few of the amazing tourist **destinations** that have their beginnings in the world's Fair!

a UFO: an alien space ship or "unidentified flying object"

revolving: moving in a circle

a destination: a place you travel to

Grammar for Writing

The Simple Present Tense: Negative Statements

To make negative statements with *be*, add *not* after *am/is/are*.

Be (Negative)	
I am **not**	we are **not**
you are **not**	you (plural) are **not**
he / she / it is **not**	they are **not**
✗ You not at school today.	
✓ You are not at school today.	

NOTE: You can form contractions with *is/are* and *not*.

| is not = isn't | are not = aren't |
| there is not = there isn't | there are not = there aren't |

To make negative statements with other verbs, use *do not* and *does not*.

I	**do not**	have live go	we	**do not**	have live go
you	**do not**	have live go	you (plural)	**do not**	have live go
he she it	**does not**	have live go	they	**do not**	have live go
✗ Vegetarians not eat meat.					
✓ Vegetarians do not eat meat.					
✗ He do not goes to my school.					
✓ He does not go to my school.					

NOTE: You can form contractions with *do / does* and *not*.

do not = don't   does not = doesn't

ACTIVITY 12   Changing Verbs from Affirmative to Negative

Change the verb in each sentence from the affirmative to the negative. Also write the contraction form.

1. I have a car.

   I do not (don't) have a car.

2. The capital of Japan is Osaka.

   _____

3. Jeremy goes to the library every day.

   _____

4. There is a Thai restaurant on Green Street.

   _____

5. Angel Falls is in Brazil.

   _____

6. Kate and Julia are roommates.

   _____

7. Jeff and Michael work at the gas station.

   _____

8. There are answers in the back of the book.

   _____

9. The teacher wants a new computer.

   _____

10. Olivia bakes cookies every Saturday.

   _____

ACTIVITY 13 **Practicing Possessive Adjectives**

Think about the answers to these questions. Then write the answers using complete sentences. Use a possessive adjective three times.

1. What is your best friend's first name?

   My best friend's first name _____

2. What is your best friend's last name?

   _____

3. Where is your best friend from?

   _____

4. How big is your best friend's family?

   _____

5. Why is this person your best friend?

   _____

6. What job does your best friend want to do in the future?

   _____

Write your sentences from Activity 13 in paragraph form. Give your paragraph a title, and remember to indent the first line.

Grammar for Writing

Simple Sentences

A **simple sentence** is a sentence that has only one subject-verb combination. Most simple sentences have one subject and one verb.

Japan imports oil from Saudi Arabia.

However, simple sentences can have a subject-verb combination that has more than one subject and/or more than one verb.

Subject(s)	Verb(s) + Other information
Japan	imports oil from Saudi Arabia.
Japan and **Germany**	import oil from Saudi Arabia.
Japan	imports oil and exports cars.
Japan and **Germany**	import oil and export cars.
Japan	exports cars and technology.
Japan and **Germany**	export cars and technology.

NOTE: All of these sentences are simple sentences because they have only one subject-verb combination.

Compound Sentences

A **compound sentence** is a sentence that has two simple sentences that are joined by a **connecting word** (such as *and*). A compound sentence has <u>two</u> separate subject-verb combinations.

Subject 1 + Verb 1	Comma	Connecting Word	Subject 2 + Verb 2
Japan <u>imports</u> oil	,	and	**Saudi Arabia** <u>imports</u> vegetables.
Jack <u>likes</u> Italian food	,	but	**he** <u>prefers</u> Thai food.
Abbie <u>watched</u> TV last night	,	so	**she** <u>did not finish</u> her homework.
We <u>can travel</u> to the mountains	,	or	**we** <u>can go</u> to the beach.

IMPORTANT: Compound sentences *always* use a comma (,) and a connecting word to connect two sentences.

ACTIVITY 15 Identifying Sentence Types

For each sentence, circle the subject(s) and underline the verb(s). Then write *S* (simple sentence) or *C* (compound sentence).

1. __*C*__ Japan's (flag) is red and white, and Canada's (flag) is also red and white.

2. __*S*__ (Japan and Canada) have the same two colors in their flags.

3. _____ The weather is bad, but the airplane will leave on time.

4. _____ It is extremely hot in Abu Dhabi during the summer.

5. _____ This map of Europe, Africa, and Asia is very old.

6. _____ You can have cake or ice cream for dessert.

7. _____ The students take a test every Friday, but they do not like it!

8. _____ January, March, May, July, August, October, and December have 31 days.

9. _____ This recipe requires two cups of flour, two cups of sugar, and one cup of milk.

10. _____ Ian and Carlos like surfing and skiing.

11. _____ Some people prefer gold rings, but I prefer silver rings.

12. _____ These silver and gold rings are different in weight, so they are different in price.

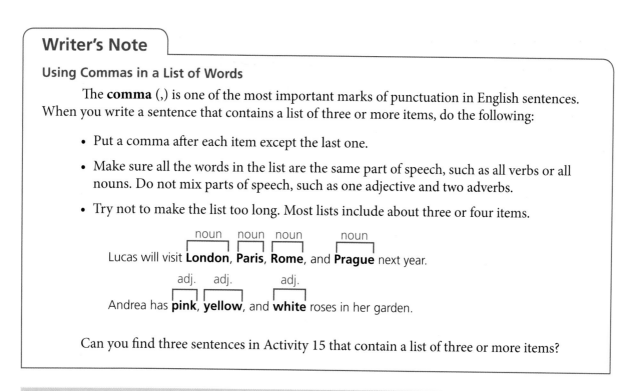
There are more comma rules on pages 232–233 in the *Brief Writer's Handbook*.

Grammar for Writing

Connecting Words in Compound Sentences

Connecting Word	Meaning	
	1st sentence	**2nd sentence**
and	Gives information.	Adds (similar) information.
but	Gives information.	Adds contrasting (different) information.
so	Tells about something.	Tells about the result of (what happened because of) the event or information in the 1st sentence.
or	Describes a choice (option 1).	Describes another choice (option 2).

There are more connecting words on page 244 in the *Brief Writer's Handbook*.

ACTIVITY 16 Combining Simple Sentences into Compound Sentences

Combine each pair of simple sentences into one compound sentence. Use a comma and a connecting word: *and, but, or,* or *so.* Some sentences can be connected with more than one connecting word. Be prepared to explain your choice.

1. Seher lives in Turkey. Seher's sister lives in Canada.

   _____

2. Carlos works on Saturday. He cannot come to the movies with us.

   _____

3. We go to school every day. We play tennis on weekends.

   _____

4. Luis and Kathy are related. They are not brother and sister.

   _____

5. Hurricanes begin in the Atlantic Ocean. Typhoons begin in the Pacific.

   _____

6. I like to go to the beach in the summer. My brother prefers to hike in the mountains.

_____

7. I do not feel well. I will call the doctor.

_____

8. You can watch television. You can watch a movie.

_____

Grammar for Writing

Using *A* and *An* with Count Nouns

A **count noun** is a noun that you can count. A count noun has a singular form (such as *phone*) and a plural form (such as *phones*). A **non-count noun** has only one form (such as *rice*).

Follow these rules for using *a/an* with singular count nouns:

- Use *a* or *an* in front of a singular count noun when the noun is general (not specific).

- Use *a* in front of a singular count noun that begins with a <u>consonant</u> sound.

- Use *an* in front of a singular count noun that begins with a <u>vowel</u> sound.

There is information on exceptions to these rules for words beginning with *h* and *u* on page 237 in the *Brief Writer's Handbook*.

Non-count Nouns	Count Nouns	
	Singular	**Plural**
money	**a** dollar	twenty dollars
ice	**an** ice cube	ice cubes
information	**a** number	numbers
clothing	**a** blue shirt	blue shirts
vocabulary	**a** word	fifteen words
bread	**a** slice of bread	slices of bread
honesty	**an** honest person	honest people
homework	**an** assignment	three assignments

IMPORTANT: Forgetting to put *a* or *an* in front of a singular count noun is a grammatical mistake.

✗ Will made <u>sandwich</u>.

✓ Will made a sandwich.

✗ There is a bank<u>s</u>.

✓ There is a bank. / There are banks.

✗ Sara has information<u>s</u>.

✗ Sara has <u>an</u> information.

✓ Sara has information.

When there is an adjective before a singular count noun, *a / an* agrees with the first letter of the adjective, not the noun.

✗ Our friends attend a excellent school.

✓ Our friends attend an excellent school.

✗ Erica eats an red apple every day.

✓ Erica eats a red apple every day.

There is a list of common non-count nouns on page 238 in the *Brief Writer's Handbook*.

ACTIVITY 17 Using Count and Non-count Nouns

For each item, decide if the noun is a count noun or a non-count noun. Write *C* (count noun) or *NC* (non-count noun). Then circle all the noun forms that can be used in the sentence below.

This is _____.

1. __C__ (a cat)	cats	a cats	cat
2. __NC__ a ice	an ice	(ice)	ices
3. _____ moneys	a money	money	a moneys
4. _____ breads	bread	a breads	a bread
5. _____ an eraser	a eraser	erasers	an erasers
6. _____ homeworks	a homework	a homeworks	homework
7. _____ an unit	units	a unit	an units
8. _____ country	a country	an country	a countries
9. _____ information	informations	an information	a information
10. _____ a happiness	happiness	happinesses	an happiness
11. _____ word	a word	words	a words
12. _____ an present	a presents	presents	a present
13. _____ a answer	answers	an answers	an answer
14. _____ politician	politicians	a politician	a politicians

ACTIVITY 18 Using *A* and *An* in Sentences

Rewrite each sentence. Add *a* or *an* if necessary.

1. My father has stressful job.

_____

2. You have visitor today.

_____

3. The teacher gives us homework every day.

_____

4. There is large cake in the kitchen.

_____

5. His mother is elegant woman.

_____

6. I am sorry. I do not have time to talk to you right now.

_____

7. We take tests in this class every week.

_____

8. Their sister is great cook!

_____

9. You can buy good furniture in that store.

_____

10. This soup needs salt.

_____

Correct the paragraph. There are 13 mistakes. The first mistake has been corrected for you.

2 adjective mistakes   2 verb mistakes   3 capitalization mistakes

2 punctuation mistakes   1 article mistake   2 possessive adjective mistakes

1 subject pronoun mistake

Example Paragraph 42

Not an Average Teenager

Steven Mills is not your **typical** athletic teenager. Steven is an
gymnast, and he want to compete in the olympics. He wakes up at five
o'clock in the morning every day because he has to practice before school.
First, he has a breakfast healthy. Then she jogs to the National Gymnasium
on Cypress street. He practices gymnastics for two hours. Then he gets ready
for school. Steven goes to school from eight-thirty in the morning until
three o'clock in the afternoon. After school, he returns to the Gymnasium
for classes special with him coach. When practice finish at six o'clock, Steven
returns home. He eats dinner, does his homework and talks with their
family. Steven is in bed early to be ready to work hard again the next day.

typical: average;
regular

Building Better Sentences: For further practice with the sentences and paragraphs in this unit, go to
Practice 3 on page 254 in Appendix 1.

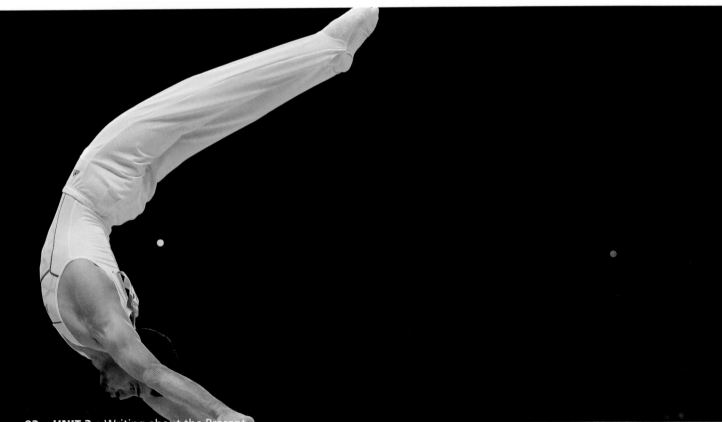

Building Better Vocabulary

ACTIVITY 20 **Word Associations**

Circle the word or phrase that is most closely related to the word or phrase on the left. If necessary, use a dictionary to check the meaning of words you do not know.

	A	B
1. successful	negative effect	positive effect
2. an entrepreneur	to be the boss	to have a boss
3. part-time	to work forty hours	to work twenty hours
4. engineering	bridges	orchestras
5. typical	normal	rare
6. a sibling	a brother	an uncle
7. forever	an end	no end
8. servers	an office	a restaurant
9. to separate	to divide	to mix
10. professional*	a nice suit	shorts and a t-shirt
11. to wake up	to go to sleep	to stop sleeping
12. traditional*	new	old
13. stressful*	an earthquake	a picnic
14. athletic	a library	a soccer field
15. requires*	must have	optional

*Words that are part of the Academic Word List. See pages 245–246 for a complete list.

ACTIVITY 21 Using Collocations

Fill in each blank with the word that most naturally completes the phrase on the right. If necessary, use a dictionary to check the meaning of words you do not know.

1. make / take   to _____ a friend

2. make / take   to _____ a shower in the morning

3. from / with   to be separated _____ your family

4. at / on   to wake up _____ six in the morning

5. desk / mistake   a common _____

6. in / on   to compete _____ a game

7. in / on   to write _____ the whiteboard

8. of / to   a map _____ the region

9. see / watch   to _____ a television show

10. get / take   to _____ information for a report

ACTIVITY 22 Parts of Speech

Study the word forms. Fill in each blank with the best word form provided. Use the correct form of the verb. If necessary, use a dictionary to check the meaning of words you do not know. (NOTE: The word in bold is the original word that appears in the unit.)

Noun	Verb	Adjective	Sentence Practice
friend / friend<u>ship</u> (A PERSON) / (A THING)	Ø	**friend<u>ly</u>**	1. My best _____ lives in Mexico. 2. It is important to be _____ to others.
profess<u>ion</u> / profession<u>al</u> (A THING) / (A PERSON)	Ø	**profession<u>al</u>**	3. Computer graphics is a popular _____. 4. Her _____ experience is impressive.
separat<u>ion</u>	**separate**	separate	5. I _____ my clothes before washing them. 6. Jessica and her husband drive _____ cars.
visit<u>or</u> / visit (A PERSON) / (A THING)	**visit**	Ø	7. Wake up! There is a _____ waiting to see you. 8. Every Sunday, Maria _____ her sister.
prefer<u>ence</u>	**prefer**	prefer<u>red</u>	9. Lisa has a _____ for spicy foods. 10. Ian _____ to go to the beach for his vacations.

Noun endings: *-ship, -ion, -al, -tion, -or, -ence*
Adjective endings: *-ly, -al, -ed*

Original Student Writing

Original Writing Practice

Think about your favorite sport. Then follow these steps for writing about the sport. Put a check (✓) next to each step as you complete it. When you finish your paragraph, use the checklist that follows to edit your work.

_____ STEP 1: In your first sentence, write: _____ *is my favorite sport.* Fill in the blank with the name of the sport.

_____ STEP 2: In your next sentence, write about the first reason you like the sport. Next, write a sentence with an explanation about why you like it.

_____ STEP 3: In the next sentence, write about the second reason that you like the sport. Next, write a sentence with an explanation for this reason.

_____ STEP 4: In the next sentence, write about the final reason that you like the sport. Next, write a sentence with an explanation for this reason.

_____ STEP 5: In the last sentence, give your general opinion about this sport.

_____ STEP 6: Use subject and object pronouns in two of the sentences in STEPS 2 through 4.

_____ STEP 7: Use a possessive adjective in one sentence in STEPS 2 through 4.

_____ STEP 8: Use at least two of the vocabulary words or phrases presented in Activity 20, Activity 21, and Activity 22. Underline these words or phrases in your paragraph.

_____ STEP 9: Go back and look at your sentences. Combine two simple sentences to make one compound sentence.

If you need ideas for words and phrases, see the Useful Vocabulary for Better Writing on pages 247–249.

☑ Checklist

1. ❏ I checked that each sentence has a subject and a verb.

2. ❏ I used the correct tense for all verbs.

3. ❏ I began every sentence with a capital letter.

4. ❏ I capitalized all proper nouns (names, cities, countries, etc.).

5. ❏ I ended every sentence with the correct punctuation.

6. ❏ I used commas correctly in compound sentences.

7. ❏ I gave my paragraph a title.

Exchange papers from Activity 23 with a partner. Read your partner's paragraph. Then use Peer Editing Sheet 3 on NGL.Cengage.com/GW1 to help you comment on your partner's paragraph. Be sure to offer positive suggestions and comments that will help your partner improve his or her writing. Consider your partner's comments as you revise your own paragraph.

Additional Topics for Writing

Here are ten ideas for journal writing. Choose one or more of them to write about. Follow your teacher's directions. (We recommend that you skip a line after each line that you write. This gives your teacher a place to write comments.)

PHOTO
TOPIC: Look at the photo on pages 70–71. Write about your typical routine for a day of the week. Include the time that you usually wake up, what you eat for breakfast, what your activities are during the day, whom you spend your time with, how you enjoy the day, and what time you go to bed.

TOPIC 2: Choose a member of your family. Write a paragraph about this person. Give general information. Include the person's name, age, nationality, job, hobbies, etc.

TOPIC 3: Write about a special city in a particular country. Include the name of the city, the special tourist attractions, and why it is a special city for you.

TOPIC 4: Write about a job that interests you. Include the title of the job, the duties of the job, and why it is interesting to you.

TOPIC 5: What is your favorite Web site? Write about a Web site that you like. What is the address? What kind of information does it have? Why do you like it?

TOPIC 6: Write about your favorite teacher this semester. What is his / her name? What subject does he / she teach? What makes this teacher special?

TOPIC 7: Write about a restaurant that you like. What is the name of this restaurant? Why do you like it? What kind of food does it serve? What is the price range? How is it decorated?

TOPIC 8: Write about your favorite movie. What is the title? Who are the main actors in the movie? What is the story about? Why do you like this movie?

TOPIC 9: Write about a specific food that you know how to cook without using a cookbook. What are the ingredients? Is it easy to prepare? Are the ingredients expensive?

TOPIC 10: Write about a type of music that you do *not* enjoy. Why don't you like it? How does it make you feel when you hear it?

Timed Writing

How quickly can you write in English? There are many times when you must write quickly, such as on a test. It is important to feel comfortable during those times. Timed-writing practice can make you feel better about writing quickly in English.

1. Take out a piece of paper.

2. Read the writing prompt below.

3. Brainstorm ideas for five minutes.

4. Write eight to ten sentences.

5. You have 20 minutes to write.

Describe a typical "free day." What do you normally do during this free time? Who do you like to spend your time with?

_____

_____

_____

_____

_____

_____

_____

_____

_____

_____

_____

_____

_____

For more practice with the grammar, vocabulary, and writing found in this unit, go to NGL.Cengage.com/GW1.

People decided to paint their homes
bright colors in Itilleq, Greenland.

OBJECTIVES To learn the simple past tense of *be* and regular verbs
To learn the simple past tense of irregular verbs
To study the negative form of the simple past tense
To practice compound sentences with *but*
To study complex sentences to show time

*Can you write about the
home you lived in as a child?*

Grammar for Writing

The Simple Past Tense of *Be*

What happened yesterday? What happened 10 years ago? When we talk about actions in the past, we use the **simple past tense**. Both regular verbs and irregular verbs can be used in the simple past tense.

The most common verb in English, *be*, is an **irregular** verb.

Be	
I **was**	we **were**
you **were**	you (plural) **were**
he / she / it **was**	they **were**
✗ I am in Guatemala last year.	
✗ I were in Guatemala last year.	
✓ I was in Guatemala last year.	

The Simple Past Tense of Regular Verbs

Add *-ed* or *-d* to the end of **regular** verbs to form the simple past tense.

Visit	
I **visited**	we **visited**
you **visited**	you (plural) **visited**
he / she / it **visited**	they **visited**

Live	
I **lived**	we **lived**
you **lived**	you (plural) **lived**
he / she / it **lived**	they **lived**
✗ We call our parents yesterday.	
✓ We called our parents yesterday.	

There is more information on the spelling of regular simple past tense verbs on page 234 in the *Brief Writer's Handbook*.

Circle the regular simple past tense verbs. Then answer the questions using complete sentences.

A Great Leader

Cesar Chavez was an important **civil rights** leader in the United States. Chavez was born in Arizona to a Mexican-American family. Life was hard for his family there, so they moved to California. In California, most of the family needed to work in the fields picking lettuce. Working in the fields was difficult. His family received very little money, and people often treated them badly. Chavez stopped school in the eighth grade and started to work in the fields, too. Chavez wanted to make changes to field workers' lives. He was angry about the **discrimination** he saw. In the 1970s and 1980s, he organized many **boycotts** and **protests** against companies to **demand** better treatment for the workers. Like Gandhi and Martin Luther King, Jr., Chavez's protests were nonviolent. He often used **hunger strikes** to bring attention to his fight. Over time, thousands of people joined his peaceful cause. It was not always easy, but in his lifetime, Chavez helped to improve the lives of America's field workers.

civil rights: the legal rights that every citizen in a country has

discrimination: unfair treatment of a person because he/she belongs to a particular group

a boycott: a refusal to buy or use something as a protest

a protest: an act done to show strong disagreement about something that is wrong or unfair

to demand: to strongly ask for something, especially if you feel it is your right

a hunger strike: when a person does not eat food for a long time to protest something

Circle all of the simple past tense verbs. Then follow the directions, and make changes to the paragraph.

See Unit 2 to review subject pronouns and possessive adjectives.

Example Paragraph 44

The Top of the Class

In 2008, Antonio Salazar and Marcus Quaglio (were) the top students at the University of North Carolina. They studied in the history department. They **excelled** in their studies. In class, they answered all of their instructors' questions. Their test scores were better than the other students', and their class projects received excellent marks. When they graduated in 2012, they finished at the top of the class. All of the teachers were very proud of Antonio and Marcus.

to excel: to do something very, very well

Now rewrite the paragraph on the lines on page 105 with these changes:

1. Change the male students' names to *Fatima Al-Otaibi*. (NOTE: *Fatima* is a woman's name.)

2. Change any pronouns or possessive adjectives to go with *Fatima*.

3. Change any other words necessary (such as *students* to *student* in the first sentence).

The Top of the Class

In 2008, Fatima Al-Otaibi was the top student at the University of North Carolina.

_____

_____

_____

_____

_____

_____

_____

_____

_____

_____

_____

ACTIVITY 4 **Writing about an Important Person**

Think of an important person who lived in the past, such as a famous politician, singer, artist, or athlete. It could be a member of your family or a friend. (However, this person should not be alive.) Answer the questions using complete sentences.

1. Who was this person?

_____

2. Where was the person born?

_____

3. What was the person's job?

_____

4. Why is the person important to you? What did he or she do?

_____

_____

_____

5. How do you feel when you think about this person? Why?

_____

_____

Grammar for Writing

The Simple Past Tense of Irregular Verbs

Many verbs in English have an **irregular** past tense form. Here are some common irregular verbs.

Base Form	Simple Past	Base Form	Simple Past	Base Form	Simple Past
be	was/were	go	went	say	said
become	became	have	had	see	saw
buy	bought	leave	left	send	sent
do	did	make	made	sit	sat
eat	ate	pay	paid	speak	spoke
feel	felt	ride	rode	teach	taught
get	got	run	ran	write	wrote

| ✗ Last night, I buy a new CD. |
| ✗ Last night, I buyed a new CD. |
| ✓ Last night, I bought a new CD. |

There is no special rule that tells when a verb is irregular. You must memorize the simple past tense. A dictionary will tell you when a verb is irregular.

There is a longer list of common irregular simple past tense verbs on page 235 in the *Brief Writer's Handbook*.

ACTIVITY 5 Practicing Irregular Verbs in the Past Tense

Circle the 13 irregular simple past tense verbs. Then answer the questions using complete sentences.

Example Paragraph 46

Helen Keller (1880–1968)

Helen Keller was a famous American author. Until Keller was two years old, she was a healthy and happy child. However, when she was two years old, she became very ill with an extremely high **fever**. The fever made her **deaf** and **blind**. Because she could not communicate with anyone, she became a wild and uneducated child. When she was seven years old, her parents hired Annie Sullivan to teach Helen. After many long struggles, Sullivan taught Helen to communicate with sign language. This **achievement** opened a new world to Keller. When Helen was 20 years old, she began taking college courses. After her graduation, she wrote 13 books and traveled around the world to talk about her life. She was an incredible human being.

a fever: a high temperature in the body

deaf: not able to hear

blind: not able to see

an achievement: something important that you are able to complete on your own

Post-Reading

1. Why was Keller blind and deaf?

   _____

2. What happened when she became blind and deaf?

   _____

3. What did Annie Sullivan do for Helen?

   _____

4. What happened when Helen was 20 years old?

   _____

5. What did Helen do after she graduated?

   _____

Grammar for Writing

Time Phrases with the Simple Past Tense

Time phrases help to show that something happened in the past. Some of these time phrases include:

last night   last week   this morning   yesterday   (two minutes) ago

You can put these time phrases at the beginning or the end of a sentence. Avoid using them in the middle of a sentence.

✗ I yesterday scratched my knee.

✗ I scratched yesterday my knee.

✓ Yesterday I scratched my knee.

✓ I scratched my knee yesterday.

ACTIVITY 6 **Using Irregular Simple Past Tense Verbs**

Ask your partner the questions. Write each answer as a complete sentence. Use the irregular form of the simple past tense.

1. Where were you last summer?

_____

2. How did you feel yesterday?

_____

3. Where did you go last weekend?

_____

4. When did you last see a funny movie?

_____

5. What did you buy last week?

_____

6. Who did you speak with yesterday?

_____

7. When did you leave for school this morning?

_____

8. When did you do your homework?

_____

9. Where did you eat lunch yesterday?

_____

10. When did you last send an e-mail?

_____

Grammar for Writing

The Simple Past Tense of *Be*: Negatives

Add the word *not* to make a negative sentence with *be*.

Subject	Be + Not	Subject	Be + Not
I	**was <u>not</u>**	we	**were <u>not</u>**
you	**were <u>not</u>**	you (plural)	**were <u>not</u>**
he / she / it	**was <u>not</u>**	they	**were not**
✗ I <u>did</u> not <u>be</u> at work last night.			
✓ I was not at work last night.			

Writer's Note

Contractions with the Negative Form of *Be*

Some contractions are possible with the verb *be* in negative form.

was not = wasn't   were not = weren't

Careful! Be sure that the apostrophe (') is placed directly before the letter *t*. Remember that the apostrophe takes the place of the missing *o* in *not*.

   ✗ She <u>is'nt</u> my sister.

   ✗ She <u>isn,t</u> my sister.

   ✓ She isn't my sister. (OR She's not my sister.)

   ✗ I <u>was'nt</u> in class yesterday.

   ✗ I <u>wasn,t</u> in class yesterday.

   ✓ I wasn't in class yesterday.

It is important to remember that contractions might be too informal for academic writing. Ask your instructor if using contractions in this course is acceptable.

Practicing Negative Forms of *Be* in the Simple Past

Write the correct form of *be* in each blank. Be sure to use the negative form where indicated.

Example Paragraph 47

Moving to the United States

My name is Panadda, and I **1** _____

born in Thailand. I (**2** negative) _____ the first

child. My sister Suntri **3** _____ born three years

before I **4** _____ born. My parents (**5** negative)

_____ rich, but they **6** _____ always

happy. They **7** _____ hard workers. In 2012, we moved

to the United States. Everyone in my family **8** _____

very excited. We **9** _____ also scared. My mother

10 (negative) _____ able to speak English at all. When

we arrived, she began English classes. My sister and I started school.

We **11** (negative) _____ comfortable in the classroom

because we did not know the language. After a few years, however, we

learned the language and the culture of the United States.

Read the paragraph about Panadda's family in Activity 7 again. Think about your own family. Write a short paragraph about your family. Choose a time in the past, and use the simple past tense. Include at least one compound sentence in your paragraph.

_____

_____

_____

_____

_____

_____

_____

_____

_____

_____

_____

_____

Grammar for Writing

The Simple Past Tense: Negatives

Aside from the verb *be*, the negative form of all other verbs in the simple past is formed in the same way.

Subject	Did + Not	Base Form
I, you, he / she / it, we, you (plural), they	did not	live
		visit
		do

NOTE: Contraction: *did not = didn't*

✗ Ahmed <u>no finish</u> his homework.

✗ Ahmed <u>no finished</u> his homework.

✓ Ahmed did not finish his homework.

✗ Ella <u>no wrote</u> a report for her boss.

✗ Ella <u>did not wrote</u> a report for her boss.

✓ Ella did not write a report for her boss.

Practicing Negative Verbs in the Simple Past

Unscramble the words to make correct sentences. Change the verbs to the negative simple past tense form.

1. live / in Johannesburg in 2010 / Carmen

   Carmen did not live in Johannesburg in 2010.

2. Ling / engineering / last semester / study

   _____

3. last year / him / Humberto's parents / visit

   _____

4. large brains / have / dinosaurs

   _____

5. me / help / Juan / with my homework

   _____

6. Emma / the letter / send / this morning / to her parents

   _____

7. with his academic advisor yesterday / speak / Karl / yesterday

   _____

8. I / my homework / yesterday / do

   _____

9. the party early / Janiel and Yosemy / last night / leave

   _____

10. go / my brother / last Saturday / to the grocery store

    _____

The sentences below are false. With a partner, rewrite each sentence using the negative form of the verb to make the sentence true. Then write a correct affirmative sentence. Follow the example. NOTE: Some verbs are regular, and some are irregular.

There is a complete list of irregular verbs on page 235 in the *Brief Writer's Handbook.*

1. John F. Kennedy was a leader in Mexico.

    John F. Kennedy was not a leader in Mexico. He was a leader in the United States.

2. Confucius lived in Colombia.

    _____

3. Zinedine Zidane played professional basketball.

    _____

4. Lady Gaga sang her songs in Arabic.

    _____

5. The *Titanic* sank in the Pacific Ocean.

_____

6. Leonardo da Vinci came from Germany.

_____

7. Albert Einstein invented the radio.

_____

8. Stephen King wrote *Romeo and Juliet*.

_____

ACTIVITY 11 **Reviewing the Simple Past Tense**

Fill in the blanks with the simple past tense of the verbs in parentheses. Write the negative form where indicated.

Example Paragraph 48

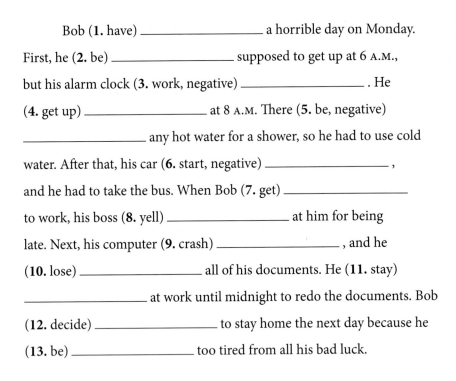

Bob's Horrible Day

Bob (**1.** have) _____ a horrible day on Monday.
First, he (**2.** be) _____ supposed to get up at 6 A.M.,
but his alarm clock (**3.** work, negative) _____ . He
(**4.** get up) _____ at 8 A.M. There (**5.** be, negative)
_____ any hot water for a shower, so he had to use cold
water. After that, his car (**6.** start, negative) _____ ,
and he had to take the bus. When Bob (**7.** get) _____
to work, his boss (**8.** yell) _____ at him for being
late. Next, his computer (**9.** crash) _____ , and he
(**10.** lose) _____ all of his documents. He (**11.** stay)
_____ at work until midnight to redo the documents. Bob
(**12.** decide) _____ to stay home the next day because he
(**13.** be) _____ too tired from all his bad luck.

Grammar for Writing

Using *But* Correctly

The connector *but* shows a contrast or difference between the ideas it connects.

Two simple sentences	I bought a car. John bought a truck.
One compound sentence	I bought a car, **but** John bought a truck.

But is not always a connector. Sometimes it is a preposition that means *except*. When *but* is used as a preposition, do not use a comma.

Compound Sentence (Use Comma)		Simple Sentence (No Comma)
We visited all the countries in South America, but we did not visit Chile.	=	We visited all of the countries in South America **but** (except) Chile.
All of the new cars are hybrid cards, but this one is not a hybrid car.	=	All of the new cars **but** (except) this one are hybrid cars.

ACTIVITY 12 **Using *But* as a Preposition**

Combine the two simple sentences into one simple sentence using *but* as a preposition (= *except*).

1. I ate all the food on my plate. I did not eat the spinach.

   _____

2. Every student in the class is wearing running shoes. Stephanie is not wearing running shoes.

   _____

3. The teacher asked everyone a question. The teacher did not ask Ryan and Joe a question.

   _____

4. My mother cleaned every room in the house. My mother did not clean my room.

   _____

5. The official language of every country in South America is Spanish. Spanish is not the official language of Brazil, Suriname, and French Guyana.

   _____

Reviewing Compound Sentences

Identify each sentence as a simple (*S*) or compound (*C*) sentence. If the sentence is compound, insert a comma where it is necessary.

1. ___S___ The girls practiced every day.

2. ___S___ They did not win the tennis tournament.

3. ___C___ The girls practiced every day, but they did not win the tennis tournament.

4. _____ The committee members made a decision but the manager did not like it.

5. _____ Neal worked with his father at the shoe store for almost twenty years.

6. _____ We went to Canada but we did not visit Toronto.

7. _____ With the recent increase in crime in that area of the city, the local residents there are worried about their safety.

8. _____ Summer is a good time to practice outdoor sports but winter is not.

9. _____ All of the workers but Marian arrived at yesterday's meeting on time.

10. _____ Saudi Arabia and Kuwait import equipment, cars, food, and medicine.

11. _____ The chairs in the living room are made of wood but the chairs in my office are made of metal.

12. _____ All of the chairs in the kitchen but this one are made of wood.

ACTIVITY 14 **Writing Compound Sentences**

Read each incorrect statement about two brothers. Then write a compound sentence with *but* that contains correct information. Use the information from the charts.

Name:	Andrew Bright
Born:	January 14, 1938
Died:	March 23, 2008
Home City:	Washington, DC
Education:	high school diploma
Work:	firefighter
Family:	wife and five children
Hobbies:	singing

Name:	Ian Bright
Born:	May 1, 1930
Died:	September 22, 2003
Home City:	Chicago, Illinois
Education:	college degree
Work:	high school math teacher
Family:	single
Hobbies:	playing baseball

1. They were born on the same day.

   Andrew was born on January 14, but Ian was born on May 1.

2. The brothers were born in the same year.

   _____

3. They both sang as a hobby.

   _____

4. Both brothers were married.

   _____

5. They lived in the same city.

   _____

6. They had the same level of education.

   _____

7. Both men had the same kind of job.

   _____

8. They died on the same date.

   _____

ACTIVITY 15 **Interviewing Your Classmates**

Ask different classmates the following questions. Write down their answers. Then use information about yourself and your classmates' answers to write compound sentences with *but*.

1. Where are you from? *Classmate's answer:* ___Peru___

   I am from Kuwait, but José is from Peru.

2. What did you eat for dinner last night? *Classmate's answer:* _____

   _____

3. Where was your last vacation? *Classmate's answer:* _____

   _____

4. Why did you come to this school? *Classmate's answer:* _____

   _____

5. What country do you want to visit? *Classmate's answer:* _____

   _____

Grammar for Writing

Sentence Variety: Complex Sentences

When you write, sentence variety is important. This will make your writing more interesting. Good writers use both **simple** and **compound sentences**. There is another way to add variety to your sentence writing: **complex sentences**.

A complex sentence is a combination of two clauses. A **clause** is a group of words that includes a subject and a verb. In a complex sentence, one clause begins with a connecting word such as *after*, *before*, *when*, *until* and *as soon as*. The other clause has no connecting word.

Simple Sentences	Clause (subject + verb)	Clause (subject + verb)
	John played tennis.	Vicky watched TV.

Compound Sentence	Clause (subject + verb)	Connector	Clause (subject + verb)
	Joe played tennis,	and	Vicky watched TV.

Complex Sentence	Clause (subject + verb)	Clause (connector + subject + verb)
	Joe played tennis	after Vicky watched TV.

Compound sentences and complex sentences both use a connector to combine two clauses. However, the connector in a compound sentence is <u>not</u> part of the clauses. In a complex sentence, the connector is part of one clause.

In a complex sentence, the clause with the connector cannot be a sentence by itself. It is a fragment and must be connected to another sentence.

   ✗ <u>Until he bought a car.</u> (**fragment**) John rode his bicycle to work.

   ✓ Until he bought a car, John rode his bicycle to work.

   ✗ My mom made dinner. <u>When my dad got home.</u> (**fragment**)

   ✓ My mom made dinner when my dad got home.

Commas in Complex Sentences

When a complex sentence begins with a clause that contains a connecting word, put a comma at the end of the clause. Do not use a comma when the connecting word is in the middle of the sentence.

   ✗ After she ate dinner she called her friend.

   ✓ After she ate dinner, she called her friend.

   ✗ She called her friend, after she ate dinner.

   ✓ She called her friend after she ate dinner.

There is more information on connectors in complex sentences on page 244 in the *Brief Writer's Handbook*.

Identify each sentence as a simple (S), compound (CD), or complex (CX) sentence. If the sentence is compound or complex, insert a comma where it is necessary.

1. _____S_____ Alexi and Juan finished their essays last night.

2. _____CD_____ Karl saw a movie this weekend, but he thought it was really boring.

3. _____CX_____ Before Mahmood left class, he spoke to the teacher about his homework.

4. _____ Amy expected to take a test today but she was wrong.

5. _____ The students did not have any questions after the teacher gave the assignment.

6. _____ My friends and I went down to the cafeteria and had lunch.

7. _____ We arrived at school early enough to get a coffee before class.

8. _____ We can study here or we can go to the library.

9. _____ I got a horrible grade on my first test but a good one this time.

10. _____ When Karen wanted information for her report she went to the library.

11. _____ We cannot take a break until we finish the project.

12. _____ Everyone but Ricky came to the study group.

13. _____ Sam began to study as soon as he got to the library.

14. _____ Ying decided to ask a friend to edit her paper and she liked her friend's comments.

Grammar for Writing

Using Complex Sentences to Show Time Order

You can use time words to show order in a sentence, for example *first, next, after that.* You can also use complex sentences with connectors such as *after* and *as soon as* to show time order. This will help add sentence variety to your writing.

After	Use this connector with the action that happened first.
With Time Words	First, Leila finished school for the day. Then she drove to work.
Complex Sentence	**After** Leila finished school for the day, she drove to work. OR Leila drove to work **after** she finished school for the day.

When	Use this connector with the action that happened first.
With Time Words	First, my sister got sick. Then the doctor gave her some medicine.
Complex Sentence	**When** my sister got sick, the doctor gave her some medicine. OR The doctor gave my sister some medicine **when** she got sick.

Before	Use this connector with the action that happened second.
With Time Words	First, Josh practiced driving. Next, he took the driver's license exam.
Complex Sentence	**Before** Josh took the driver's license exam, he practiced driving. OR Josh practiced driving **before** he took the driver's license exam.

As soon as	Use this connector with the first action when the second action happened very soon after the first action.
With Time Words	First, I arrived in Portland. Right after that, I toured the city.
Complex Sentence	**As soon as** I arrived in Portland, I toured the city. OR I toured the city **as soon as** I arrived in Portland.

NOTE: When the clause with the connector comes at the beginning of the sentence, you must use a comma after it.

ACTIVITY 17 Writing Complex Sentences in the Past

Combine the two simple sentences into a complex sentence. Use the connector in parentheses.

1. (as soon as)
   First: I graduated from high school.
   Second: I got a summer job.

   As soon as I graduated from high school, I got a summer job.

2. (before)
   First: Jack traveled around the world.
   Second: Jack began his English classes.

3. (when)
First: My sister and I finished our homework.
Second: My sister and I went to a movie.

_____

4. (after)
First: The house caught on fire.
Second: The police fire department arrived very quickly to put out the fire.

_____

5. (before)
First: The young woman looked left and right.
Second: The young woman crossed the street.

_____

6. (when)
First: The lights in the classroom went out.
Second: The teacher told the students not to worry.

_____

7. (as soon as)
First: Jacob had the freedom to study abroad.
Second: Jacob moved to California to study English.

_____

Correct the paragraph. There are 15 mistakes. (If you need help finding the mistakes, look at the numbers in parentheses. These numbers tell you how many mistakes are in each line.) The first mistake has been corrected for you.

Example Paragraph 49

Muhammad Ibn Batuta

(3)   Ibn Batuta ^was^ a famous moroccan traveler. He live in Morocco

(1)   in the fourteenth century. When he was a man young, he made a

(1)   religious trip to Mecca. However, Ibn Batuta loves to see new places

(2)   so much that he continued to travel. This was no his original plan

(1)   but he continued on his journey. He had many adventures during her

(2)   travels and he met many interesting people. After he returned home

(2)   he did not forgot about his journey. He wrote a book about his travels,

(2)   this book now gives us a lot of information important about life in

(1)   the fourteenth century. Also, gives us more information about this

(1)   interesting and important man

Building Better Sentences: For further practice with the sentences and paragraphs in this unit, go to Practice 4 on page 255 in Appendix 1.

Building Better Vocabulary

Circle the word or phrase that is most closely related to the word or phrase on the left. If necessary, use a dictionary to check the meaning of words you do not know.

	A	B
1. horrible	very bad news	very good news
2. a century	one hundred years	ten years
3. to communicate*	to keep information	to share information
4. excellent	the best	the worst

5. to continue	to not stop	to pause
6. proud	a grade of 45 percent	a grade of 100 percent
7. to discriminate*	negative action	positive action
8. to demand	to make a strong request	to make a weak request
9. to worry	to be excited	to be unhappy
10. to graduate	to complete school	to do little by little
11. the beginning	the first minute	the last minute
12. a manager	a boss	a teacher
13. original	a copy	not a copy
14. to arrive	to come to a place	to leave a place
15. to scare	to laugh	to scream

*Words that are part of the Academic Word List. See pages 245–246 for a complete list.

ACTIVITY 20 Using Collocations

Fill in each blank with the word that most naturally completes the phrase on the right. If necessary, use a dictionary to check the meaning of words you do not know.

1. before / first   the _____ thing to do

2. to / for   a trip _____ Puerto Rico

3. to / at   to arrive _____ the supermarket

4. information / communication   to share _____ about the problem

5. about / for   to have a question _____ your homework

6. against / on   to discriminate _____ someone

7. make / take   to _____ a decision

8. communication / vegetables   effective _____

9. freedom / beginning   the _____ to do anything that you want to do

10. afraid / excited   to be _____ about a new class

Study the word forms. Fill in each blank with the best word form provided. Use the correct form of the verb. If necessary, use a dictionary to check the meaning of words you do not know. (NOTE: The word in bold is the original word that appears in the unit.)

Noun	Verb	Adjective	Sentence Practice
pride	Ø	**proud**	1. She was very _____ when she graduated.
			2. I have a lot of _____ in my children.
excellence	**excel**	**excel**lent	3. Damon _____ in swimming when he was younger.
			4. That was an _____ movie!
communication	**communicate**	communica**tive**	5. We _____ by phone for three hours yesterday.
			6. Roberto was shy, but now he is more _____.
continuation	**continue**	continu**ous**/ continu**al**	7. The students _____ to study after the semester ended.
			8. The _____ traffic noise gave me a headache.
culture	Ø	cultur**al**	9. I know about Indian _____.
			10. Kim and Jo's _____ differences are small.

Noun endings: *-ence, -ion, -tion*

Adjective endings: *-ent, -ive, -ous, -al*

Original Student Writing

ACTIVITY 22 **Original Writing Practice**

Reread the paragraph about Cesar Chavez on page 101 and your answers to Activity 4 on page 105. Then think of an important person (different from the person in Activity 4) that you want to write about.

Follow the steps to write a paragraph about this person. Use the simple past tense. Put a check (✓) next to each step as you complete it. When you finish your paragraph, use the checklist that follows to edit your work.

_____ STEP 1: In your first sentence, tell the name of the person and how that person was important.

_____ STEP 2: In your next sentence, write where the person was born.

_____ STEP 3: In the next sentence, tell about the person's job.

_____ STEP 4: In the next three or four sentences, tell a short story about the person. The story should show why the person is important.

_____ STEP 5: Make one compound sentence.

_____ STEP 6: Make one complex sentence.

_____ STEP 7: Use a negative verb in one of the sentences.

_____ STEP 8: In the last sentence, write why you chose this person.

_____ STEP 9: Use at least two of the vocabulary words or phrases presented in Activity 19, Activity 20, and Activity 21. Underline these words and phrases in your paragraph.

> If you need ideas for words and phrases, see the Useful Vocabulary for Better Writing on pages 247–249.

☑ Checklist

1. ❑ I checked that each sentence has a subject and a verb.

2. ❑ I used the correct form of all the simple past tense verbs.

3. ❑ I began every sentence with a capital letter.

4. ❑ I capitalized all proper nouns (names, cities, countries, etc.).

5. ❑ I used commas correctly in compound and complex sentences.

6. ❑ I ended every sentence with the correct punctuation.

7. ❑ I gave my paragraph a title.

ACTIVITY 23　Peer Editing

Exchange papers from Activity 22 with a partner. Read your partner's paragraph. Then use Peer Editing Sheet 4 on NGL.Cengage.com/GW1 to help you comment on your partner's paragraph. Be sure to offer positive suggestions and comments that will help your partner improve his or her writing. Consider your partner's comments as you revise your own paragraph.

Additional Topics for Writing

　　　Here are ten ideas for journal writing. Choose one or more of them to write about. Follow your teacher's directions. (We recommend that you skip a line after each line that you write. This gives your teacher a place to write comments.)

PHOTO
TOPIC: Look at the photo on pages 98–99. Describe a home you lived in when you were a child. How big was the house? What color was the house? Where was the house? What did you like or dislike about the house? What was your favorite room in the house?

TOPIC 2: Describe a vacation you took. Where did you go? What did you do? Who went on this vacation with you? How old were you when you went on this trip? Did you like this vacation?

TOPIC 3: Write about a movie you saw or a book you read. Did you like it? Who was your favorite character? What was the story about? Did the author have a message for the audience of this book or movie?

TOPIC 4: Write about what you did last weekend. Where did you go? Who did you go with? Did you enjoy it? Why or why not?

TOPIC 5: Write about a person you used to know. Who was this person? Where did you meet this person? What was special about this person?

TOPIC 6: Write about an important event in your life. How old were you? What happened? Why is this event important to you?

TOPIC 7: Describe a holiday that you and your family spent together. What was the occasion? Which family members were there? What did you do?

TOPIC 8: Write about something embarrassing that happened to you. How old were you? What happened? Why were you embarrassed? Who saw this happen? How did you feel afterwards?

TOPIC 9: Write about a day you spent outdoors. What did you do? Where did you go? Who did you go with? What specific activities did you do? How was the weather?

TOPIC 10: Describe a pet you had in the past. What was the pet's name? What kind of animal was it? How long did you have this pet? Why did you like (or dislike) this pet?

Timed Writing

How quickly can you write in English? There are many times when you must write quickly, such as on a test. It is important to feel comfortable during those times. Timed-writing practice can make you feel better about writing quickly in English.

1. Take out a piece of paper.

2. Read the writing prompt below.

3. Brainstorm ideas for five minutes.

4. Write eight to ten sentences.

5. You have 20 minutes to write.

Describe a sad (or happy, frightening, funny, important, etc.) event or time from your past. What was the event or time? Give examples of how this event or time made you feel that emotion.

_____

_____

_____

_____

_____

_____

_____

_____

_____

_____

_____

_____

_____

_____

For more practice with the grammar, vocabulary, and writing found in this unit, go to NGL.Cengage.com/GW1.

People are enjoying
the night in Tokyo, Japan.

OBJECTIVES To learn the present progressive tense
To practice compound sentences with *and* and *so*
To learn complex sentences with the present
To practice adverbs of manner
To study prepositional phrases of place

Can you write about what is happening at this moment?

Grammar for Writing

The Present Progressive Tense

We use the **present progressive tense** to describe actions that are happening in the current moment or an extended period of time in the present (for example: today, this week, this semester, this year).

Subject	Be	(Not)	Verb + -ing
I	am		eating
he / she / it	is	(not)	studying
we / you / you (plural) / they	are		taking
			running
			doing

There is a list of spelling rules for verbs ending in -ing on page 236 in the *Brief Writer's Handbook.*

Stative (Non-action) Verbs

Be careful! Some verbs in English do <u>not</u> usually take the progressive tense because they are not action verbs. Here are some common **non-action**, or **stative**, verbs: *be, have, see, love, believe, own,* and *want.*

✗ I am having a new boss.

✓ I have a new boss.

✗ Mark is not wanting the gift.

✓ Mark does not want the gift.

There is more information on stative verbs on page 236 in the *Brief Writer's Handbook.*

ACTIVITY 1 Identifying the Present Progressive Tense

Underline the 17 present progressive verbs in the paragraph.

Example Paragraph 50

A Busy Tourist Site

In pictures, Machu Picchu, Peru, seems very **remote** and quiet, but it is often a very busy place! Right now, hundreds of tourists are arriving by bus and getting in line to enter the **site**. **Guards** are giving directions, and **hikers** from the Inca **Trail** are putting their heavy bags in lockers. Inside Machu Picchu, people are walking everywhere. They are looking at

remote: far away, distant

a site: a location, specific place

a guard: a person who protects another person or place

a hiker: a person who takes long walks for enjoyment

a trail: a path

the amazing **ruins** and taking lots of pictures. Guides are talking to travel groups about the history of this ancient site. Smaller groups of people are exploring the ruins by themselves. They are touching the stones and talking about the beauty all around them. One man is even touching the Sacred Rock in the northern square. Many visitors are standing in line and waiting to take a picture of themselves with the ruins in the background. Some people are walking up and down the **steep**, narrow steps and staircases very carefully. They are taking their time because the stones are wet. They do not want to fall down the slippery steps. Some adventurous tourists are walking up a mountain trail behind Machu Picchu so that they can see more of this amazing site. It is hard to believe that such an old and distant place can be so lively!

the ruins: the remains of something that is old and/or damaged

steep: going up/down at a high angle

Study the picture of Bruce and his friends. Then read the paragraph. Fill in the missing verbs based on the picture.

Example Paragraph 51

A University Student's Room

Tomorrow is a big day for Bruce. His mother is coming to visit him at college for the first time. Bruce is very excited, but he is also worried. His dorm room is a mess. This is why he called all his friends to come help him. His good friend Lina **1** _____ the floor because the carpet is very dirty. Bruce's friend Joe

2 _____ some of Bruce's clothes to the laundry. At the same time, Bruce's roommate Paul **3** _____ all of the empty pizza boxes and soda cans. Bruce **4** _____ . Bruce feels very lucky to have such good friends, and he is sure that the room will be ready for his mother's visit.

Describing a Scene

Write sentences that describe the action in the picture. Use the present progressive. Make at least one of your sentences negative.

1. _____

2. _____

3. _____

4. _____

5. _____

6. _____

7. _____

8. _____

Avoiding Repetition in Compound Sentences

When you have the same noun in both parts of a compound sentence, you should use a pronoun after the connector. This helps avoid repetition.

Repetitive Writing (Using Only Nouns)	Better Writing (Using Nouns and Pronouns)
Jake is washing the car, so **Jake** is getting wet.	**Jake** is washing the car, so **he** is getting wet.
Tia is making **a lemon cake**, and **the lemon cake** smells good.	Tia is making **a lemon cake**, and **it** smells good.

Reviewing *And* and *So* in Compound Sentences

We use *and* in a compound sentence to show added information. We use *so* in a compound sentence to show cause and effect. The sentence after *so* shows the result (what happens because) of the first sentence.

ACTIVITY 4 Practicing Compound Sentences with *And*

Match the sentences. Then combine the two sentences into a compound sentence using *and*.

Column A	Column B
~~Ann is watching television.~~	Oranges contain a lot of vitamin C.
Oranges taste great.	I hope the marigold seeds grow quickly.
Ecuador exports millions of cut flowers around the world.	~~Ann is texting her friends.~~
That blouse is the perfect color for you.	Alaska contains large amounts of oil.
I am planting marigold seeds.	Valia is making roast beef for her guests.
Alaska is a part of the United States.	That blouse matches your pants and handbag.
Valia is having guests for dinner tonight.	Colombia exports millions of cut flowers around the world, too.

1. Ann is watching television, and she is texting her friends.

2. _____

3. _____

4. _____

5. _____

6. _____

7. _____

ACTIVITY 5 Combining Sentences with *So*

In each item, identify each sentence as a cause (C) or a result (R). Then combine them into a compound sentence using *so*. Put the cause first, then the connector *so*, and then the result. Use correct punctuation.

1a. _____C_____ I am thirsty.

b. _____R_____ I am drinking a huge glass of water.

_____I am thirsty, so I am drinking a huge glass of water._____

2a. _____ We are not playing tennis.

b. _____ It is raining really hard.

_____

3a. _____ Mr. Lopez is taking Ana to the doctor.

b. _____ Ana is very sick.

_____

4a. _____ The audience loves the show.

b. _____ The audience is applauding wildly.

_____

5a. _____ Jonathan is not feeling well.

b. _____ Jonathan is not going to the party.

_____

6a. _____ I am not buying the latest smart phone.

b. _____ The latest smart phone is very expensive.

_____

7a. _____ Brian is sleeping late today.

b. _____ Brian is extremely tired.

_____

8a. _____ Angela needs to buy some fruits and vegetables.

b. _____ Angela is shopping at the farmer's market.

_____

Scenarios: Writing Compound Sentences with *So* and the Present Progressive

Write a compound sentence with *so* to describe the action happening in the picture. Use the present progressive tense.

1. _____
_____
_____
_____
_____
_____
_____

2. _____
_____
_____
_____
_____
_____
_____

3. _____
_____
_____
_____
_____
_____
_____

4. _____
_____
_____
_____
_____
_____
_____

5. _____

_____

_____

_____

_____

_____

6. _____

_____

_____

_____

_____

_____

_____

Writer's Note

Other Uses of *So*

One use of *so* is as a connector in compound sentences to show a cause and result. However, *so* has several other meanings.

In compound sentences, we use a comma with *so*, but we do <u>not</u> use a comma with the other uses of *so*.

Other Meanings of *So*	
Meaning	**Examples**
An adverb that means *very* or *extremely*	It is **so** hot today. You speak English **so** well.
A connector that means *in order to*. The full form is *so that*. *So that* is more formal than *so*, but the meaning is the same.	Lina went to the bank **so that** she could get some cash. Lina went to the bank **so** she could get some cash.
A common word at the beginning of a statement or question to continue a conversation. It is not used in academic writing.	Carlos: We were at the beach all day yesterday. Maria: **So** what time did you finally get home?

Use the picture and the prompts to write sentences. Use the present progressive tense. Then compare your sentences with a classmate's sentences.

Some fans / cheer / for their team

Other fans / wave / flags and banners

The coach / watch / the ball

The referee / run / toward the goal

The soccer ball / go / into the net

The forward / hope / the shot will be a goal

The goalkeeper / jump / for the ball

1. The soccer ball _____.

2. The goalkeeper _____.

3. The coach _____.

4. The referee _____.

5. The forward _____.

6. Some fans _____.

7. Other fans _____.

ACTIVITY 8 **Writing a Paragraph**

Rewrite the sentences from Activity 7 in paragraph form. Use your imagination and add some extra information to describe the game. Also, do the following:

- Use at least two adjectives.
- Make two compound sentences.
- Add a concluding sentence.
- Create a title for the paragraph.

Example Paragraph 52

_____

The soccer game between Blackwatch and Dynamo is very exciting. Many things are

happening right now!

_____

_____

_____

_____

_____

_____

_____

_____

Grammar for Writing

Verbs in Complex Sentences

When, while, before and *after* are connecting words that are commonly used to describe actions in the present in complex sentences.

- *While* can describe two actions that occur at the same time. You can use present progressive in each part of the sentence, or you can use present progressive in one clause and simple present in the other. There is no difference in meaning.

    Mark <u>is listening</u> to music **while** he <u>is surfing</u> the Internet.
    Mark <u>is listening</u> to music **while** he <u>surfs</u> the Internet.

- *When, after,* and *before* help describe the time order of activities in the present. The simple present tense (not present progressive) is most often used in both clauses.

    Mark <u>listens</u> to music **when** he <u>surfs</u> the Internet.
    After Mark <u>finishes</u> his homework, he <u>watches</u> television.
    Before Mark <u>goes</u> to bed, he <u>brushes</u> his teeth.

REMEMBER: When a connecting word begins the sentence, put a comma at the end of the clause. Do not use a comma when the connecting word is in the middle of the sentence.

Go back and look at your paragraph about the soccer game in Activity 8. Can you add a complex sentence to it?

ACTIVITY 9 **Practicing Complex Sentences in the Present**

Ask a partner the questions. Write his or her answers using a complex sentence. Use the appropriate connecting word.

1. What are you doing while you are sitting in class?

   _____

2. What do you usually do when you wake up?

   _____

3. After you eat breakfast in the morning, what do you do?

   _____

4. What do you do when you are not at school?

   _____

5. While you are completing your classwork, what is your teacher doing?

   _____

ACTIVITY 10 Identifying Sentence Types

Identify each sentence as a simple (*S*), compound (*CD*), or complex (*CX*) sentence. If the sentence is compound or complex, insert a comma where necessary.

1. ___S___ My brother and I are hiking and fishing this weekend.

2. ___CD___ The motorcycle is in the garage, and the car is in the driveway.

3. ___CX___ When Harry and Darlene went to the picnic yesterday, they got sunburns.

4. _____ I always think about my question before I ask the teacher.

5. _____ You are learning so many new words.

6. _____ A noun is a word like *sandwich* and a verb is an action word such as *eat*.

7. _____ While we are studying we are learning new material.

8. _____ After Kelly checks her e-mail she works for two hours.

9. _____ Lisana is working for a computer company but she does not have a computer engineering degree.

10. _____ I make a pot of coffee when I wake up in the morning.

11. _____ The capital of Argentina is Buenos Aires and it is the most populated city in the country.

12. _____ The traffic was terrible so Lance missed his plane.

Grammar for Writing

Adverbs of Manner

Adverbs are words that describe or give more information about verbs, adjectives, and other adverbs. There are several kinds of adverbs in English. **Adverbs of manner** usually describe verbs. They tell <u>how</u> an action is done.

Kerry picked up the baby **carefully.**   (*How* did Kerry pick up the baby? **carefully**)

My sister is studying **hard.**   (*How* is my sister studying? **hard**)

Adverbs of manner usually end in -*ly*.

Common Adverbs of Manner					
quickly	easily	nervously	carefully	happily	slowly
suddenly	quietly	badly	fast*	hard*	well*

*These adverbs do not use the -*ly* form.

Be careful! There are a few words that end in –*ly* that are adjectives, not adverbs.

friendly   deadly   lovely   lonely

REMEMBER: Adjectives describe nouns. The baby is <u>happy</u>. Ben is a <u>happy</u> baby.

Go back and look at your paragraph about the soccer game. Can you add adverbs to describe the action?

ACTIVITY 11   Using Adverbs

Fill in each blank with an adverb that describes the action of the underlined verb. Use an adverb from the list of common adverbs of manner above or use your own.

1. Julia <u>is studying</u> _____ in the library.

2. He <u>got onto</u> the bus _____ because it was raining.

3. Mariah <u>spoke</u> _____ at the conference. Everyone was impressed by her speech.

4. David <u>is doing</u> _____ in this class. He never studies!

5. Nili <u>cried</u> very _____ during the movie. I didn't know she was crying until I looked at her.

6. Teresa <u>typed</u> the letter _____. I thought she would never finish.

7. Nate <u>read</u> the directions _____. He did not want to make a mistake.

8. I had a cold, so I <u>did not play</u> _____ at the soccer game last week.

9. Maria and Faisal <u>passed</u> the test _____ because they <u>studied</u> _____ for it.

10. Will <u>opened</u> the door _____ because he was afraid to wake up the baby.

Grammar for Writing

Prepositional Phrases of Place

A **prepositional phrase** is a phrase that begins with a preposition and includes a noun or pronoun. The noun or pronoun is called the **object of the preposition**.

prepositional phrase = preposition + object of preposition (noun / pronoun)

One type of prepositional phrase is the **prepositional phrase of place.** A prepositional phrase of place:

- tells about location—it answers the question *Where?*

- functions like an adverb—it modifies a verb

Parts of a Prepositional Phrase (of Place)				
Prepositional Phrase	**Preposition**	**Article** (a, an, the) **Demonstrative Determiner** (this, that, these, those) **Possessive Adjective** (my, your, her, etc.) **Quantifier** (some, any, one, two, etc.) Ø	**Adjective** Ø	**Noun** **Pronoun**
at the picnic	at	the		picnic
on that little table	on	that	little	table
next to my friends	next to	my		friends
under two old chairs	under	two	old	chairs
near them	near			them

It is common to put place phrases at the end of a sentence.

✗ We ate at the picnic lots of salad.

✓ We ate lots of salad at the picnic.

✗ Loretta in my house lives.

✓ Loretta lives in my house.

Prepositional Phrases of Place and Time Words

In sentences where you have a prepositional phrase of place <u>and</u> a time word or phrase, use this rule:

At the end of a sentence, place phrases usually come <u>before</u> time words or phrases.

Less Common: | time words | place phrase
Meet me **tomorrow afternoon in the library.**

More Common: | place phrase | time words
Meet me **in the library tomorrow afternoon.**

Less Common: | time words | place phrase
She saw him **at 2 P.M. at the bank.**

More Common: | place phrase | time words
She saw him **at the bank at 2 P.M.**

Also Correct: | time words | place phrase
At 2 P.M., she saw him **at the bank.**

There is more information on prepositions on page 242 in the *Brief Writer's Handbook*.

ACTIVITY 12 **Practicing with Place Phrases and Time Words**

Unscramble the words to make correct sentences. Be sure to use the correct form of the verb. Use correct capitalization and punctuation.

1. Ashley / right now / drive / to the hospital

   _____

2. this semester / the Silva sisters / at City College / a grammar class / take

   _____

3. at the car dealership / today / a new car / we / buy

   _____

4. at the gym / exercise / Janie / this morning

   _____

5. we / take / today / in Mrs. Wang's class / an important test

   _____

6. put / Eric / right now / his books / in the trunk of his car

7. at the moment / eat dinner / Luis / at a restaurant

_____

8. Sara / a pie / now / put / in the oven

_____

9. I / at the moment / busy / be / at work

_____

10. the squirrels / now / nuts / bury / under our oak tree

_____

ACTIVITY 13 **Writing What You See: Describing Actions**

Write a paragraph based on observation. Choose a place to observe people—for example, a park, a mall, or a cafeteria. You may also use a show on television or an illustration in a magazine. Choose a situation or place that has several people who are doing different actions. Follow these instructions:

- Look at the people. What are they doing?

- Write about an object. What is happening with it?

- Use the connectors *and* and *so* if possible.

- Use one or two adverbs of manner.

There is a lot of action happening right now.

_____

_____

_____

_____

_____

_____

_____

_____

_____

_____

_____

ACTIVITY 14 **Editing: Grammar and Sentence Review**

Correct the paragraph. There are 13 mistakes.

2 compound sentence mistakes	2 capitalization mistakes	2 adverb mistakes
2 complex sentence mistakes	2 adjective mistakes	2 verb mistakes
1 mistake with time words		

Example Paragraph 53

The Squirrel

A small red squirrel climbing a tree. He is a young squirrel. His tail is twitching **nervously** and his nose is moving quick. I think he is searching for food. The squirrel red is right now on a long tree branch. He wants to jump to another tree. The squirrel hears something so he looks down. he is coming down from the tree tall. When he reaches the ground he runs to a few pieces of chocolate chip cookie. These cookie pieces lying on the grass. the squirrel is walking toward the food and **inspecting** it. The squirrel grabs the cookie and **stuffs** it in his mouth. While he is eating his tail is moving rapid. The little red squirrel is now happy.

nervously: in a worried or frightened way

to inspect: to look at carefully to learn more about it

to stuff: to quickly and carelessly put something into one's mouth

Building Better Sentences: For further practice with the sentences and paragraphs in this unit, go to Practice 5 on page 255 in Appendix 1.

Building Better Vocabulary

ACTIVITY 15   **Word Associations**

Circle the word or phrase that is most closely related to the word or phrase on the left. If necessary, use a dictionary to check the meaning of words you do not know.

	A	B
1. remote	close	far
2. a site*	an idea	a place
3. thirsty	to need food	to need water
4. to hear	with your ears	with your eyes
5. a carpet	a garage	a rug
6. steep	at an angle	flat
7. younger	18 years old	80 years old

	A	B
8. a mess	not organized	very organized
9. slippery	safe	unsafe
10. a piece	a coin	a part
11. to climb	to go near	to go up
12. a tail	a body part	a story
13. to inspect*	to look at	to wait for
14. to stuff	to fill	to empty
15. empty	a lot inside	nothing inside

*Words that are part of the Academic Word List. See pages 245–246 for a complete list.

ACTIVITY 16 **Using Collocations**

Fill in each blank with the word that most naturally completes the phrase on the right. If necessary, use a dictionary to check the meaning of words you do not know.

1. line / step   to be in a _____

2. feel / have   to _____ very lucky

3. about / on   to be worried _____

4. delicious / dirty   to wash _____ clothes at the laundry

5. ancient / angle   to see an _____ site

6. picnic / sunburn   to get a _____

7. cleaner / machine   a vacuum _____

8. party / mess   to make a _____

9. monkey / room   an empty _____

10. nervous / powerful   to get _____ about something

Study the word forms. Fill in each blank with the best word form provided. Use the correct form of the verb. If necessary, use a dictionary to check the meaning of words you do not know. (NOTE: The word in bold is the original word that appears in the unit.)

Noun	Verb	Adjective	Sentence Practice
beauty	Ø	beautif<u>ul</u>	**1.** I saw a _____ sunset yesterday.
			2. That painting is a thing of _____.
luck	Ø	**luck<u>y</u>**	**3.** The _____ lottery winner won $5 million.
			4. It was bad _____ that our team lost the game.
thirst	Ø	**thirst<u>y</u>**	**5.** If you are _____, drink some water.
			6. Keith is playing tennis. He is probably suffering from _____.
fish<u>ing</u>	fish	Ø	**7.** _____ is a relaxing sport.
			8. We _____ in the lake behind our house.
hik<u>ing</u> / hik<u>er</u> (A THING) (A PERSON)/	hike	Ø	**9.** The _____ carefully climbed up the steep trail.
			10. Ian _____ in the forest on the weekends.

Noun endings: *-ing, -er*
Adjective endings: *-ful, -y*

Original Student Writing

Imagine that you are a TV news reporter. Right now you are at the location of an emergency situation (for example, a traffic accident, a building on fire, the scene of a natural disaster).

- Write a paragraph that describes what is happening.
- Use your imagination.
- You may use a picture from a newspaper, magazine, or the Internet to help your imagination.

Follow these steps for writing. Put a check (✓) next to each step as you complete it. When you finish your paragraph, use the checklist on the next page to edit your work.

_____ STEP 1: In your first sentence, tell where you are and what you are watching.

_____ STEP 2: In your next sentence, describe the person/people or thing(s) you see. Use adjectives to give a clear idea to your reader.

_____ STEP 3: In the next two to four sentences, describe what the people are doing.

_____ STEP 4: Use one or two adverbs in the sentences in STEP 3.

_____ STEP 5: Use *and* or *so* in one of the sentences. Remember to use a comma to separate the two clauses.

_____ STEP 6: Use a complex sentence with *when* or *while*.

_____ STEP 7: In the next sentence, write what you believe the people are thinking or feeling at this moment.

_____ STEP 8: In the final sentence, write your opinion about the situation.

_____ STEP 9: Use at least two of the vocabulary words or phrases presented in Activity 15, Activity 16, and Activity 17. Underline these words and phrases in your paragraph.

_____ STEP 10: Create a title for your work, and write it above the paragraph.

> If you need ideas for words and phrases, see the Useful Vocabulary for Better Writing on pages 247–249.

☑ Checklist

1. ❑ I checked that each sentence has a subject and a verb.

2. ❑ I included two subjects and verbs (two clauses) in my compound sentences.

3. ❑ I used the present progressive verbs correctly.

4. ❑ I began every sentence with a capital letter.

5. ❑ I used commas correctly in compound and complex sentences.

6. ❑ I ended every sentence with the correct punctuation.

7. ❑ I gave my paragraph a title.

ACTIVITY 19 Peer Editing

Exchange papers from Activity 18 with a partner. Read your partner's paragraph. Then use Peer Editing Sheet 5 on NGL.Cengage.com/GW1 to help you comment on your partner's paragraph. Be sure to offer positive suggestions and comments that will help your partner improve his or her writing. Consider your partner's comments as you revise your own paragraph.

Additional Topics for Writing

Here are ten ideas for journal writing. Choose one or more of them to write about. Follow your teacher's directions. (We recommend that you skip a line after each line that you write. This gives your teacher a place to write comments.)

PHOTO
TOPIC: Look at the photo on pages 128–129. Imagine that you are in a large city like Tokyo, Toronto, London, Istanbul, or Seoul. Walk around the city and write down the things that you see. What is happening in this large city?

TOPIC 2: Watch several minutes of a television program. Describe what is happening in the show.

TOPIC 3: Describe how your life is now. Include your studies, your living arrangements, and your free time.

TOPIC 4: Imagine that you are a private investigator. Imagine that you are watching a specific character or person. Write down everything that the person is doing for five minutes.

TOPIC 5: Find a picture in a magazine. Choose a picture of many people who are doing different things. Describe what each person is doing.

TOPIC 6: Imagine that you are visiting the zoo. What are the other visitors doing? Write about what the different kinds of animals are doing.

TOPIC 7: Imagine that you are walking down the street, and you see your favorite movie star walk into a café. Follow this person. What is he/she doing?

TOPIC 8: Write a letter to your friend explaining what you are doing in this class. Tell about the assignments that you have and the writing skills that you are practicing.

TOPIC 9: If you have a pet, watch it closely for ten minutes. What is it doing? Where is it going? Is it playing? Jumping? Making noise?

TOPIC 10: Imagine that you are a news reporter for a movie magazine. You are at a famous awards ceremony. What are the people doing? Name some of the famous actors. (This word means male and female actors.) What are they doing? What are they wearing? What are they saying to their friends? What are they thinking?

Timed Writing

How quickly can you write in English? There are many times when you must write quickly, such as on a test. It is important to feel comfortable during those times. Timed-writing practice can make you feel better about writing quickly in English.

1. Take out a piece of paper.

2. Read the writing prompt below.

3. Brainstorm ideas for five minutes.

4. Write eight to ten sentences.

5. You have 20 minutes to write.

Describe an exciting (or boring, interesting, etc.) activity that you are doing this year. What is the activity? What are you doing to complete it? Give as many details as possible.

_____

_____

_____

_____

_____

_____

_____

_____

_____

For more practice with the grammar, vocabulary, and writing found in this unit, go to NGL.Cengage.com/GW1.

Writing about the Future

Astronaut Tracy Caldwell Dyson looks out of the window of the International Space Station.

BJECTIVES To learn the simple future tense with *be going to* and *will*
To practice time words to show the future
To learn complex sentences in the future
To study articles *a, an,* and *the*
To use *because* in complex sentences

**Can you write about what
you think will happen in
the future?**

Grammar for Writing

The Simple Future Tense: *Be Going To*

We use the **simple future tense** to talk about future events. One way to express the simple future tense is to use ***be going to***. You can use *be going to* for:

- plans that are already made
- predictions (guesses about the future) that are about the possible result of actions that are happening in the present

Subject	Be Going To		Verb (Base Form)
I	am		eat
he / she / it	is	going to	study
			buy
we / you / you (plural) / they	are		listen

✗ I am going to a sandwich for lunch.

✓ I am going to buy a sandwich for lunch.

✗ According to the radio report, the weather going to be severe tonight.

✓ According to the radio report, the weather is going to be severe tonight.

ACTIVITY 1 Making Predictions

Make a prediction about the actions in each picture. Write complete sentences using the correct form of *be going to*.

1. _____
   _____
   _____
   _____
   _____
   _____

2. _____
   _____
   _____
   _____
   _____
   _____

3. _____
   _____
   _____
   _____
   _____
   _____
   _____

4. _____
   _____
   _____
   _____
   _____
   _____
   _____

5. _____
   _____
   _____
   _____
   _____
   _____
   _____

6. _____
   _____
   _____
   _____
   _____

Answer the questions about Michael's schedule for next week. Use complete sentences.

Sunday	Monday	Tuesday	Wednesday	Thursday	Friday	Saturday
meet Mom & Dad for lunch	meeting with Mr. Anderson	appointment with Mr. & Mrs. Pinter at the office	business report due to Ms. Simms	buy groceries	dinner with Andrea	play soccer with the guys

1. What is Michael going to do on Sunday?

   _____

2. Who is going to come to Michael's office on Tuesday?

   _____

3. On what day are Michael and Andrea going to have dinner?

   _____

4. When is Michael going to meet with Mr. Anderson?

   _____

5. What is he going to do on Thursday?

   _____

6. What are Michael and his friends going to do on Saturday?

   _____

7. What is he going to give to Ms. Simms on Wednesday?

   _____

Writer's Note

Avoiding *Gonna* in Writing

Speakers of English often pronounce *going to* as *gonna* in informal speech. However, do not use *gonna* in academic writing. You must write out the words completely.

✗ I'm gonna buy a new shirt.

✓ I am going to buy a new shirt.

Grammar for Writing

The Simple Future Tense: *Will*

Another way to express the simple future tense is to use **will**. You can use *will* for:

- future plans/decisions that are made at the moment of speaking (no planning)
- strong predictions (strong guesses about the future)
- promises and offers to help

Subject	*Will*	Verb (Base Form)
I you he / she / it we you (plural) they	will	eat study buy run listen

✗ I will opens the door for you.
✓ I will open the door for you.

✗ They will are watch a new movie tonight.
✓ They will watch a new movie tonight.

✗ We will be love each other forever.
✓ We will love each other forever.

Using Adverbs of Frequency with *Will*

Adverbs of frequency describe how often an action happens. Some examples are *always, sometimes, often, rarely,* and *never*. When you use frequency adverbs with *will*, put the frequency adverb between *will* and the main verb.

✗ My parents always will help me.
✓ My parents will always help me.

✗ The teacher will give us sometimes homework.
✓ The teacher will sometimes give us homework.

ACTIVITY 3 **Writing about the Future Using *Will***

Make five predictions about what your life will be like in ten years. Use *will* in the sentences. Use a frequency adverb in two sentences.

1. _____

2. _____

3. _____

4. _____

5. _____

Grammar for Writing

Time Words and Phrases

Good writers include **time words** and **time phrases** in their writing. Time words and phrases give important information about *when* something happens.

Common Time Words and Phrases			
first	in a minute	tomorrow	next week
next	later	next Saturday	next year
then	before that	next January	next time
finally	after that		

These time words usually occur at the very beginning or the very end of a sentence. When the time words and phrases occur at the beginning of a sentence, a comma is usually used.

We are going to go to the movies **on Saturday**.

On Saturday, we are going to go to the movies.

The airline will produce a new kind of jet **in the next few months**.

In the next few months, the airline will produce a new kind of jet.

We are going to paint the kitchen **first**.

First, we are going to paint the kitchen.

NOTE: *Then* is not followed by a comma.

ACTIVITY 4 · Practicing with Time Words

Fill in the missing time words from the word bank. One word can be used twice. Add commas where necessary.

> then   next   first   after   Sunday   finally

Example Paragraph 54

A Reunion to Remember

This year's family reunion will be special because we are going to celebrate my Aunt Laura's 98th birthday. **1** _____ everyone in our family is going to travel to my aunt's town for the weekend. The **2** _____ night, we are going to meet at Aunt Laura's house and eat a delicious dinner. **3** _____ dinner, we are going to bring out a delicious birthday cake.

4 _____ we will sing to her and give her presents. She is going to love it! The **5** _____ day, the whole family will meet in the city park for a lovely picnic. There will be food, games, and music for everyone. Aunt Laura will give a nice speech to the family, too. On **6** _____ everyone will go to lunch with Aunt Laura. **7** _____ our special celebration will be over, and everyone will return home dreaming about next year's reunion.

Review the sentences you wrote about Michael's schedule in Activity 2. Put them in correct time order, starting with Sunday. Write the sentences in paragraph form below. Use some time words to help organize your sentences.

Example Paragraph 55

Michael's Busy Schedule

Michael is going to be a very busy man next week. First, he is going to meet his mom and dad for lunch on Sunday.

Finally, he is going to play soccer with his friends on Saturday. Michael is the busiest man I know!

Writer's Note

Will vs. *Be Going To*

Will and *be going to* are both ways to form sentences about the future. There are certain situations when a writer may use only *will* or only *be going to* because the situation has a specific meaning. However, *will* and *be going to* can often be used to talk about future with little or no difference in meaning.

When writing an essay or a report, remember that *will* is more formal and more common in academic writing than *be going to*. As you write, be careful to consider whether the situation requires using *will*, *be going to*, or either.

Underline the 10 future tense verbs in the paragraph below. (Hint: Two of them might be difficult to find.) Then answer the questions that follow using complete sentences.

Carmen's Fifteenth Birthday

Next week, Carmen Viera will be 15 years old, and her family has plans for a special celebration for her. On her birthday, Carmen is going to wear a beautiful white **gown**. First, she is going to go to church with her family and friends. After church is over, they will go to an **elegant ballroom**. Then they are going to have a party called a *quince* there. When Carmen arrives, she will perform some formal dances with her friends. After that, everyone is going to dance, eat, and celebrate. Carmen can **hardly** wait. She knows that she will always remember her special day.

a gown: a long, formal dress

elegant: graceful; refined

a ballroom: a large room where formal parties are held

a *quince*: the Spanish word for *fifteen*; a traditional Latin birthday party that celebrates when a girl becomes a woman

hardly: almost not; with difficulty (a negative word)

Post-Reading

1. How old will Carmen be next week?

_____

2. What is Carmen going to wear on her birthday?

_____

3. What is the first thing she is going to do on her birthday?

_____

4. Where will they hold her _quince_ party?

_____

5. What will Carmen and her friends do at the party?

_____

Grammar for Writing

The Simple Future Tense: Negatives

Add the word _not_ to make the simple future tense (_be going to_ and _will_) negative.

Subject	Be	Not	Going To	Verb (Base Form)
I he / she / it we / you / you (plural) / they	am is are	**not**	going to	eat study buy run listen
✗ Sara not going to take me to the airport on Sunday. ✓ Sara is not going to take me to the airport on Sunday. ✗ Brett and Erica no going to play soccer tomorrow. ✓ Brett and Erica are not going to play soccer tomorrow.				

Subject	Will	Not	Verb (Base Form)
I you he / she / it we you (plural) they	will	**not**	eat study buy run listen
✗ They will not to come to the party. ✓ They will not come to the party. ✗ The president not make a speech on television tonight. ✓ The president will not make a speech on television tonight. ✗ My company will don't give me a raise this year. ✓ My company will not give me a raise this year.			

ACTIVITY 7 **Changing Affirmative to Negative**

Rewrite the affirmative sentences as negative sentences, and rewrite the negative sentences as affirmative ones. Write out the entire sentence.

1. There will not be a test on this information soon.

_____

2. Our friends are not going to meet us at the mall this weekend.

_____

3. Angela is going to leave for work soon.

_____

4. Our plane will leave the airport on time.

_____

5. I am going to write an e-mail to my friends back home.

_____

6. The temperature will drop sharply this evening.

_____

7. That little boy will not eat his spinach.

_____

Answer the questions.

1. What is one important thing that you are going to do in your life?

   _____

   _____

2. How long will it take to do it?

   _____

3. What are you going to do to reach this goal? Write at least three things.

   _____

   _____

   _____

   _____

4. How will you feel when you reach this goal? Why?

   _____

   _____

Grammar for Writing

Verbs in Complex Sentences about the Future

Use the simple present tense and the simple future tense with complex sentences about the future.

Clause 1 (Simple Future)	Clause 2 (Connector + Simple Present)
Calvin **is going to take** a nap	<u>after</u> he **finishes** his work.
Those birds **will fly** south	<u>before</u> the weather **becomes** too cold.

Clause 1 (Connector + Simple Present)	Clause 2 (Simple Future)
<u>If</u> we **do not leave** now,	we **will be** late.
<u>When</u> Maya **gets** home,	she **is going to read** a good book.

Do <u>not</u> use the simple future tense in both clauses.

    ✗ When the rain <u>is going to stop</u>, I am going to rake the leaves.

    ✓ When the rain stops, I am going to rake the leaves.

    ✗ The police will arrest a passenger on the plane after Flight 873 <u>will arrive</u> in Paris.

    ✓ The police will arrest a passenger on the plane after Flight 873 arrives in Paris.

Identify each sentence as a simple (*S*), compound (*CD*), or complex (*CX*) sentence. If the sentence is compound or complex, insert a comma if necessary.

1. _____S_____ I am going to go surfing next weekend.

2. _____CD_____ My father is going to retire next year, but my mother is going to continue working.

3. _____CX_____ After Gerardo finishes painting, his house will look beautiful.

4. _____ Irene is going to call you when she gets home from work.

5. _____ Brett and his friends are going to go to the hockey game and cheer for their team.

6. _____ Ariel is going to go to college next year but her brother is going to get a job.

7. _____ When the game is over we are going to eat at Harvey's Grill.

8. _____ I will bring a salad and dessert to the party.

9. _____ Leslie and Serena will be roommates next semester but they do not get along very well.

10. _____ If we do not finish this project on time the company will lose the contract.

11. _____ Ana and her friends will not be able to go to the museum this weekend.

12. _____ We are going to visit our family in Mexico City next weekend.

Writing Complex Sentences in the Future

Answer each question using a complex sentence with connectors such as *after, before, when, until,* and *as soon as.* Use the correct verb tense in each clause.

1. What are you going to do after you graduate?

   _____

2. What are you going to do as soon as you finish this activity?

   _____

3. What will you not do before you go to bed tonight?

   _____

4. When are you going to do your homework?

   _____

5. When will you finish all your English courses?

   _____

6. What are you going to do after you eat dinner?

   _____

Writer's Note

Using the Future Tense in Academic Writing

Writers may use the future to make a prediction about the information in their academic writing. Therefore, it is common to find the future tense in the last sentence of a paragraph. The future can also be used to describe a process. However, it is rare to find an entire academic paragraph that only uses the future tense.

Grammar for Writing

The Indefinite Articles: *A/An*

    A, an, and *the* are three of the shortest words in English, but they are also three of the most important words. These words are called **articles**. They are very important in correct writing and speaking.

    The **indefinite articles** *a* and *an* can only be used with singular count nouns. In Unit 3, you learned the following rules:

- Use *a* or *an* in front of a singular count noun when the noun is general (not specific).
- Use *a* in front of a singular count noun that begins with a <u>consonant</u> sound.

- Use *an* in front of a singular count noun that begins with a <u>vowel</u> sound. Some words beginning with *h* and *u* have exceptions to this rule.

- When there is an adjective before a singular count noun, *a/an* agrees with the first letter of the adjective, not the noun.

    I bought **a** sweater.

    Luis is going to eat **a** red apple.

    Wendy has **an** elegant home.

> There is information on exceptions to these rules for words beginning with *h* and *u* on page 237 in the *Brief Writer's Handbook.*

The Definite Article: *The*

The definite article *the* can be used with both singular and plural count nouns and also with non-count nouns.

- Use *the* for the second (and third, fourth, etc.) time you talk about something.

    I bought a sweater and a coat yesterday. **The sweater** is made of wool, but **the coat** is made of leather. **The sweater** was cheap, but **the coat** was expensive.

- Use *the* when the speaker and the listener both know about or are familiar with the subject.

    My brother called and said, "I'm locked out of **the house**."

- Use *the* when the noun you are referring to is unique—there is only one. This thing can be natural or manmade.

    The Sun and **the Earth** are both in **the Milky Way Galaxy**.

    The Eiffel Tower is a beautiful monument.

    I am going to visit **the Sidney Opera House** next summer.

    The New Caledonia Barrier Reef is an important home for green sea turtles.

> There is a more complete list of when to use the article *the* on pages 237–238 in the *Brief Writer's Handbook.*

Article Use Summary

When Your Meaning Is:	Singular Count Nouns	Plural Count Nouns	Non-count Nouns
General	a / an	Ø*	Ø*
Specific	the	the	the

*Ø means "do not use an article."

> There is a short list of common non-count nouns on page 238 in the *Brief Writer's Handbook.*

Using Modifiers with Singular Count Nouns

A non-count noun (*water, honesty*) and a plural count noun (*cars, women*) can be used alone in a sentence. However, a singular count noun (*car, woman*) cannot be used alone in a sentence. These words must <u>always</u> be preceded by a modifier (a word that gives more information about the noun):

- an article (*a, an, the*)
  - ✗ April owns <u>computer</u>.
  - ✓ April owns a computer.

- a possessive adjective (*my, your, his*)
  - ✗ I am <u>reading book</u>.
  - ✓ I am reading my book.

- a quantifier (*one, another, some*)
  - ✗ Give me <u>spoon</u>. This one is dirty.
  - ✓ Give me another spoon. This one is dirty.

There are more examples of quantifiers on page 240 in the *Brief Writer's Handbook*.

ACTIVITY 11 **Practicing Articles**

Fill in the blanks with *a, an,* or *the*. If no article is needed, write Ø.

Example Paragraph 57

A World Traveler

Robert likes to travel a lot, and next year he is going to go on

1 _____ excellent trip. **2** _____ trip is going to be

to Egypt and New Zealand. He wants to meet **3** _____

many new people and try **4** _____ interesting food. While

he is in Egypt, he is going to see **5** _____ Great Pyramids

at Giza and **6** _____ Sphinx of Cheops. He wants to take

7 _____ cruise down **8** _____ Nile River, but

it is probably going to be too expensive. After he visits Egypt, he will

fly to New Zealand to visit **9** _____ cousin who lives there.

10 _____ his cousin's name is Thomas. Robert and Thomas

are going to hike along the coast of New Zealand for a few weeks.

They want to see **11** _____ tuatara. Tuataras are lizards

from **12** _____ ancient reptile family. Because tuataras are

nocturnal, it is going to be difficult to see them. Finally, they will take

13 _____ bike trip on **14** _____ country's North

Island. **15** _____ trip will **definitely** be memorable!

nocturnal: active at night

definitely: without any doubt or question; surely

ACTIVITY 12 Review: Sentence Writing

Write complete sentences using the words below. Do not change the order of the words. Add the correct article(s) (*a, an, the*) where necessary. Use the correct verb tense, punctuation, and capitalization.

1. robert / not go / to / beach / tomorrow

   _____

2. laura's parents / visit / taj Majal / in india / next month

   _____

3. we / have / grammar test / next week

   _____

4. weather / be / very / nice / for / picnic / this saturday

   _____

5. kate and brad / meet / friend / for dinner / tomorrow

   _____

6. I / lend / you / some money / until / you / get your paycheck

   _____

7. this / computer / not work / anymore

   _____

8. I / bring / apple pie / for dessert

_____

9. after nicholas / graduate next week / his sister / give him / expensive gift

_____

10. my dad / meet / me / at airport / when / I / arrive / from algeria

_____

Grammar for Writing

Complex Sentences with *Because*

How would you answer this question: *Why did you decide to study English?*

One common way to answer a *why* question is to use a complex sentence with the connector *because*.

Clause 1: Includes Part of the Question	Clause 2: *Because* + Reason (Answer)
They are going to study English	**because** they want to learn a second language.
	because they want to study in an English-speaking country.
	because they like the way it sounds.

Fragments with *Because*

In formal writing, the *because* clause must be part of a complex sentence; it cannot be used as a stand-alone sentence. If the *because* clause is used as a stand-alone sentence, it is a fragment and is a mistake.

(fragment)
✗ We are not going to go to the beach. Because it is raining.

(complex sentence)
✓ We are not going to go to the beach because it is raining.

(fragment)
✗ Megan is going to go to the bookstore. Because she needs to buy a book.

(complex sentence)
✓ Megan is going to go to the bookstore because she needs to buy a book.

Because can also be used at the beginning of a sentence. When it is, you must put a comma at the end of the *because* clause.

✗ Because his brother broke the computer Alan got angry.

✓ Because his brother broke the computer, Alan got angry.

ACTIVITY 13 Identifying Sentences vs. Fragments

Identify each group of words as a complete sentence (*S*) or a fragment (*F*). If it is a complete sentence, add correct capitalization and punctuation.

1. __S__ Dante passed the test because he studied hard.

2. __F__ because the weather was so bad on Saturday evening

3. _____ because it will be cold in the mountains we are packing our heavy jackets

4. _____ because everyone will have a wonderful time at the party

5. _____ because he is going to forget about his appointment

6. _____ she is going to arrive late because her car broke down

7. _____ because I live in new york I go to the theater on broadway often

8. _____ because some committee members will not attend the conference

9. _____ the computers are going to be down today because a storm knocked out the power

10. _____ because the managers are out of the office we are going to postpone the meeting

ACTIVITY 14 Writing Sentences with *Because*

Answer each question using a complex sentence with *because*. Use the correct verb tense.

1. Why are you studying English?

   _____

2. Why is soccer a popular sport?

   _____

3. Why is fast food becoming popular around the world?

   _____

4. Why are you going to study in the library for your next test?

   _____

5. Why do some people like to drive fast?

_____

6. Why do you like your hobby?

_____

7. Why do you write letters to your family?

_____

8. Why did you skip breakfast this morning?

_____

9. Why do children learn to print before they learn cursive writing?

_____

10. Why did the man stop at the food cart?

_____

Writer's Note

Paying Attention to Commas

It is very important to pay attention to commas in your writing. Ask yourself _why_ you are using a comma in the sentence. If you cannot explain the rule, the comma probably does not belong in the sentence. Every time you write, take a moment to review all your commas.

There is a list of common comma rules on pages 232–233 in the _Writer's Brief Handbook_.

ACTIVITY 15 Practicing Comma Rules

For each item, combine the two sentences into one sentence. Remember the comma rules for compound sentences, complex sentences, and lists. You may have to change or delete some words. Be prepared to explain the comma rule that you use.

1. At the party, we ate food. We talked with our friends, and we played games.

_____

_____

_____

2. First, we are going to go to the store. Then we are going to make dinner.

_____

_____

_____

3. John wants to go to the movies. Rob and Theo want to go home.

_____

_____

_____

4. I lived in Lahore when I was a child. Lahore is in Pakistan.

_____

_____

_____

5. Elizabeth will not ride roller coasters. Roller coasters are too scary.

_____

_____

_____

Editing: Grammar and Sentence Review

Correct the paragraph. There are 11 mistakes.

2 capitalization mistakes   4 missing commas
1 adjective mistake   1 misused comma
2 missing verbs   1 misused article

Example Paragraph 58

My Winter Vacation

My winter vacation is going to be wonderful, because I am going to go to quebec. I am going to go there with my best friend. We going to spend one week in the city, and then we are going to explore the countryside for a week. I have the aunt who lives there, and she going to show us all the sights beautiful. We do not speak french very well so we are a little bit nervous. After I arrive in Canada I am going to buy a lot of souvenirs for my parents brother and friends. I cannot wait for my vacation to begin!

Building Better Sentences: For further practice with the sentences and paragraphs in this unit, go to Practice 6 on page 256 in Appendix 1.

Building Better Vocabulary

ACTIVITY 17 **Word Associations**

Circle the word or phrase that is most closely related to the word or phrase on the left. If necessary, use a dictionary to check the meaning of words you do not know.

	A	B
1. a reunion	many animals	many friends
2. presents	attendance	gifts
3. a speech	you can eat it	you can hear it
4. to celebrate	to have fun	to have problems
5. formal	very common	very proper
6. to forget	I cannot graduate	I cannot remember
7. hardly	very difficult	almost not at all
8. angry	a negative feeling	a positive feeling
9. to hike	to run	to walk
10. honesty	lies	truth
11. few	not near	not many
12. ancient	very new	very old
13. nocturnal	awake during the day	awake at night
14. a vacation	a time for fun	a time for work
15. a cousin	your uncle's child	your mother's child

ACTIVITY 18 **Using Collocations**

Fill in each blank with the word that most naturally completes the phrase on the right. If necessary, use a dictionary to check the meaning of words you do not know.

1. building / vacation   an ancient _____

2. about / for   to forget _____ something

3. between / along   to drive _____ the coast of Nova Scotia

4. sight / animal   a nocturnal _____

5. honest / unique   a(n) _____ experience

6. ballroom / speech   an informative _____

7. formal / honest   this is a(n) _____ event

8. sights / souvenirs   to visit all the _____

9. honest / angry   to get _____

10. speech / cruise   to attend a _____

ACTIVITY 19 **Parts of Speech**

Study the word forms. Fill in each blank with the best word form provided. Use the correct form of the verb. If necessary, use a dictionary to check the meaning of words you do not know. (NOTE: The word in bold is the original word that appears in the unit.)

Noun	Verb	Adjective	Sentence Practice
anger	anger	**angry**	**1.** She is going to be _____ when I tell her the news.
			2. The children _____ their mother yesterday.
honesty	Ø	honest	**3.** Please give me an _____ answer.
			4. _____ is the best policy.
nerve / nervou<u>ness</u>	Ø	**nervous**	**5.** Ben was _____ about taking the exam.
			6. I can see the _____ in her expression.
formali<u>ty</u>	formal<u>ize</u>	**formal**	**7.** The dance next week is going to be _____.
			8. Meeting the new university president is only a _____.
unique<u>ness</u>	Ø	**unique**	**9.** The _____ of the Hungarian language makes it difficult to learn.
			10. The style of Emma's dress is definitely _____.

Noun endings: *-y, -ness, -ity*
Verb ending: *-ize*
Adjective ending: *-y*

Original Student Writing

ACTIVITY 20 **Original Writing Practice**

Reread the paragraph on Carmen Viera in Activity 6 on page 161. Then review your answers to Activity 8 on page 164. Use the information from Activity 8 to write about an event that is going to happen to you in the future.

Follow these steps for writing. Put a check (✓) next to each step as you complete it. When you finish your paragraph, use the checklist that follows to edit your work.

_____ STEP 1: In your first sentence, tell who you are and what you are going to do in the future.

_____ STEP 2: In the next two sentences, give more details to describe what you are going to do.

_____ STEP 3: In the next four or five sentences, describe how you are going to achieve this goal.

_____ STEP 4: In the last sentence, tell why it is important for you to achieve this goal. (Use the word *because* in the final sentence.)

_____ STEP 5: Use time words, such as *after* and *as soon as*, in some of your sentences in STEP 3.

_____ STEP 6: Write at least one compound and one other complex sentence in your paragraph.

_____ STEP 7: Use at least two of the vocabulary words or phrases presented in Activity 17, Activity 18, and Activity 19. Underline these words and phrases in your paragraph.

If you need ideas for words and phrases, see the Useful Vocabulary for Better Writing on pages 247–249.

☑ Checklist

1. ❑ I used *be going to* or *will* when talking about the future.

2. ❑ I used articles correctly in my sentences.

3. ❑ I used commas correctly.

4. ❑ I checked that each sentence has a subject and a verb—there are no fragments!

5. ❑ I gave my paragraph a title.

ACTIVITY 21 **Peer Editing**

Exchange papers from Activity 20 with a partner. Read your partner's paragraph. Then use Peer Editing Sheet 6 on NGL.Cengage.com/GW1 to help you comment on your partner's paragraph. Be sure to offer positive suggestions and comments that will help your partner improve his or her writing. Consider your partner's comments as you revise your own paragraph.

Additional Topics for Writing

Here are ten ideas for journal writing. Choose one or more of them to write about. Follow your teacher's directions. (We recommend that you skip a line after each line that you write. This gives your teacher a place to write comments.)

PHOTO TOPIC: Look at the photo on pages 152–153. Write about what you think will happen in the future. For example, write about the future of space travel. What planets are humans going to visit? What things are going to be discovered in space? Do you think that humans will be able to live on other planets?

TOPIC 2: Write about something that you plan to do in the next two weeks. Include the people who are going to be with you, where you are going to be, and why you are going to do this.

TOPIC 3: Write about something that you plan to do in the next six months. Be sure to include where this activity is going to happen, who is going to be with you, and why you chose this activity.

TOPIC 4: Choose a current topic in the news. Read about it. Then write about what you think will happen and tell why.

TOPIC 5: Think about a special project or event that is going to happen in your neighborhood, city, or country. What is going to happen? When will it happen? Why is it happening? When will this project finally be completed?

TOPIC 6: Write about what you are going to do before you return home today. Make a list: Who are you going to be with? Are you going to do this thing (or these things) for work, school, or pleasure? How long is it going to take you to complete these things?

TOPIC 7: Describe what your wedding will be like. How big will the wedding party be? Who will be there? Where will it happen?

TOPIC 8: Describe the job you want to have when you finish school. What kind of job is it? What are your responsibilities going to be in this job? Are you going to work for a company or for yourself? How much money are you going to earn in this job?

TOPIC 9: Write about what you plan to study (your major) in college. Why did you choose this subject? What classes are going to be easy for you, and what classes are going to be difficult? How long is it going to take you to get your degree?

TOPIC 10: Describe what life is going to be like in the year 2050. What new things are going to be available? How is life going to be better than it is now? How is life going to be worse than it is now?

Timed Writing

How quickly can you write in English? There are many times when you must write quickly, such as on a test. It is important to feel comfortable during those times. Timed-writing practice can make you feel better about writing quickly in English.

1. Take out a piece of paper.

2. Read the writing prompt below.

3. Brainstorm ideas for five minutes.

4. Write eight to ten sentences.

5. You have 20 minutes to write.

Describe something that you plan to do next year. Be sure to include who is going to be with you, where it is going to happen, and why you are going to do this.

_____

_____

_____

_____

_____

_____

_____

_____

_____

_____

For more practice with the grammar, vocabulary, and writing found in this unit, go to NGL.Cengage.com/GW1.

Writing Complex Sentences with Adjective Clauses

A gorilla and chimpanzee that were orphaned as babies are examining leaves at the Lake Erova Mammal Orphanage in Gabon.

BJECTIVES To study how to add sentence variety
To learn how to write sentences with adjective clauses
To study modals

Can you write about someone or something you like?

The Importance of Sentence Variety

It is important that the sentences in a paragraph have variety. If they do not, the paragraph can be boring to read. Using compound sentences and complex sentences will make your paragraph more interesting than using only simple sentences.

An Exercise: Recognizing Sentence Variety

Each of the following paragraphs contains similar information about tennis terms. However, one of the paragraphs sounds better than the other two. Read the three paragraphs. Which one do you think is the best? Why?

Example Paragraph 59A

Tennis Terms

Tennis has many special terms. Most people do not know what these terms mean. One special word is *love*. In tennis, *love* means "nothing" or "zero." Another word is *deuce*. *Deuce* is a special term. *Deuce* means the score is tied at three points for each player. Another term is *volley*. A volley is a shot. Usually a player runs to the net to try to end the point. The player hits the ball before it touches the ground. *Love*, *deuce*, and *volley* are special words.

Number of words: 86   **Number of sentences:** 12

Tennis Terms

Tennis has many special terms. Tennis players understand these terms. Some people do not play tennis. Most of these people do not have any idea about the meaning of these terms. *Love* has a special meaning in tennis. For example, in tennis, *love* means "nothing" or "zero." Another word is *deuce*. When tennis players use this word, it means each player has three points. In other words, *deuce* means the score is tied at three points for each player. Another term is *volley*. A volley is a shot. The player hits this shot before the ball touches the ground. Usually a player runs to the net to try to end the point. The player hits the ball before it touches the ground. *Love, deuce,* and *volley* are special words. All tennis players certainly know these words.

Number of words: 136   **Number of sentences:** 16

Tennis Terms

Tennis has many special terms that tennis players know. Most people who do not play tennis do not understand the meaning of these terms. For example, one special word is *love*. In tennis, *love* means "nothing" or "zero." Another word that tennis players use is *deuce*. *Deuce* is a special term that means each player has three points. In other words, *deuce* means the score is tied at three points for each player. Another term that is used by tennis players is *volley*. A volley is a shot that the player hits before the ball touches the ground. Usually a player runs to the net to try to end the point. The player hits the ball before it touches the ground. *Love, deuce,* and *volley* are special words that all tennis players certainly know.

Number of words: 134   **Number of sentences:** 12

Evaluating the Paragraphs

Here are one teacher's comments about these three example paragraphs.

Example 1: _Many sentences are short and choppy. The information doesn't flow smoothly or connect well. Here are some poor sentences from Example 1:_

Deuce is a special term.

Another term is *volley*.

A volley is a shot.

Example 2: _This paragraph is better. For example, this complex sentence is an improvement._

When tennis players use this word, it means each player has three points.
However, there are still a few short, choppy sentences. Some information is repeated in different sentences. Here are some poor sentences from Example 2:

Tennis has many special terms. Tennis players understand these terms.

Another term is *volley*. A volley is a shot.

Example 3: _Did you think this is the best paragraph? Well, it is. The sentence combinations and variety are much better. Here are some good sentences from Example 3:_

Deuce is a special term that means each player has three points.

Another term that is used by tennis players is *volley*.

A volley is a shot that the player hits before the ball touches the ground.

Grammar for Writing

Sentence Variety: Recognizing Sentences with Adjective Clauses

One way to add sentence variety is by combining two simple sentences into a complex sentence by using an **adjective clause**. (Remember: A clause is *any* group of words that includes a subject and a verb. A sentence, for example, is a clause.)

An adjective clause:

- is a subject-verb combination that describes a noun (just like an adjective does)
- often begins with *who* or *that*
- comes directly <u>after</u> the noun it describes

Using *Who* vs. *That*

When the Adjective Clause Describes:	Use:
a person	*who* (more academic)
	that (less academic)
an animal, place, or thing	*that*
✗ I bought a fish <u>who</u> is orange and white.	
✓ I bought a fish that is orange and white.	
Acceptable: Many people that watch basketball on TV also watch football.	
Preferable: Many people **who** watch basketball on TV also watch football.	

Draw a circle around the noun that is being described by each adjective clause. Fill in the blanks with *that* or *who*.

An Old Family Photo

This is an old photo of my family. In fact, this is a photo

1 _____ was taken about eighty years ago. I remember

the old sofa **2** _____ was in my parents' living room.

The two women **3** _____ are sitting on the sofa are my

grandmother and my mother. The woman **4** _____ has

curly hair is my grandmother. The woman **5** _____ has long

hair is my mother. The little boy **6** _____ is on the sofa is

Uncle Franco. The sofa in the picture is very old. In fact, this is the sofa

7 _____ my grandmother received from her mother years

before. The man **8** _____ is sitting next to my grandmother

is my grandfather. The two men **9** _____ are behind my

grandfather and grandmother are my father and Uncle Alberto. The cat

10 _____ you see next to the sofa was my mother's pet.

The name **11** _____ my mother gave her cat was Butterball

because it was such a big fat cat. This picture is very important to me

because all of the people that I love the most are in it. **Certainly**, this is a

picture **12** _____ I will **cherish** for many more years.

certainly: without a
doubt; definitely

to cherish: to treat
with tenderness

185

Grammar for Writing

Sentence Variety: Writing Adjective Clauses

Follow these steps to write a complex sentence using an adjective clause.

1. Choose the noun you want to describe.

2. Write *who* or *that* after the noun.

3. Write a short clause that describes the noun.

Adjective Clause: *That / Who* as Subject		
That / Who (= Subject)	Verb	
who	is	very well-known

Two sentences: Joe met a **man**. The **man** is very well-known.

adjective clause

One sentence: Joe met a **man** who is very well-known.

Adjective Clause: *That / Who* as Object			
That / Who (= Object)	Subject	Verb	
that	I	remember	the most from school

Two sentences: The **subject** is science. I remember **this subject** the most from school.

adjective clause

One sentence: The **subject** that I remember the most from school is science.

An adjective clause must be connected to a sentence. An adjective clause by itself is a fragment.

✗ There is a movie. That I want to watch.

✓ There is a movie that I want to watch.

✗ The girl who goes to our school.

✓ The girl who goes to our school is very smart.

ACTIVITY 2 Combining Sentences: Adjective Clauses at the End of a Sentence

In each item, combine the two sentences into one by using an adjective clause. Change the second sentence into an adjective clause that begins with *who* or *that*. The adjective clause should describe the **boldfaced** noun.

1. The hula hoop is a **toy**. This toy became popular in the 1960s.

The hula hoop is a toy that became popular in the 1960s.

2. New Hampshire is a small **state**. This small state is in the northeastern part of the United States.

_____

_____

3. Romansch is a **language**. This language comes from Latin.

_____

_____

4. Bolivia is a South American **country**. This country does not have a coastline.

_____

_____

5. Nasi lemak is a Malaysian **dish**. This dish uses white rice and coconut milk.

_____

_____

6. Dante Alighieri was an Italian **writer**. He wrote _The Divine Comedy_.

_____

_____

7. A meerkat is a **rodent**. It is a native of Africa.

_____

_____

8. The _Titanic_ was a **ship**. It sank in the North Atlantic Ocean in 1912.

_____

_____

9. A coach is a **person**. This person trains athletes to perform well in sports.

_____

_____

10. The Burj Al Arab is a famous **building**. It is on the coast of Dubai.

_____

_____

In each item, combine the two sentences into one by using an adjective clause. Change the second sentence into an adjective clause that begins with *who* or *that*. (You will need to delete words from the second sentence.) The adjective clause should describe the **boldfaced** noun.

1. The Guatemalan **dish** is called chilaquiles. I like this food the best.

    The Guatemalan dish that I like the best is called chilaquiles.

2. The **movie** was *Spiderman*. We saw this movie on television last night.

    _____

    _____

3. The **day** was October 11. We arrived in Texas on this day.

    _____

    _____

4. The **number** was incorrect. Paul gave me this number.

    _____

    _____

5. The **story** was extremely interesting. Samir told this story.

    _____

    _____

6. The homework **assignment** was difficult. The grammar teacher gave us the homework assignment.

    _____

    _____

7. The **man** is my friend. The man is standing on the street corner.

    _____

    _____

8. The **food** got cold. We bought the food for dinner.

    _____

    _____

9. The **police officer** was very polite. The police officer gave me a speeding ticket.

    _____

    _____

10. The **play** is very popular in London. We are going to see this play tonight.

_____

_____

ACTIVITY 4 **Identifying Adjective Clauses in a Paragraph**

Underline the three sentences that have an adjective clause.

Example Paragraph 61

A Possible Problem with the Schools

The school district in our city has a problem. The teachers who work in the city's schools say they might **go on strike**. The problem is money. The teachers want to go on strike because they get **salaries** that are very low. They say the salaries are not fair, so they want the school **officials** to **raise** teachers' salaries. There will be an emergency meeting of the school board this evening, and the public is invited. The teachers hope the people who attend the meeting will agree with them about the low salaries. Will the teachers go on strike? We are going to learn the answer to this question at tonight's meeting.

to go on strike: to protest by not working

a salary: money that a person earns

an official: a director; a leader

to raise: to make higher

Copy the three sentences that you underlined in Activity 4 on the lines below. Then write the simple sentences that were combined to make the complex sentence.

Sentence 1: _____

_____

a. _____

b. _____

Sentence 2: _____

_____

a. _____

b. _____

c. _____

Sentence 3: _____

_____

_____

a. _____

_____

b. _____

ACTIVITY 6 **Combining Sentences: Adjective Clauses in Paragraphs**

Each paragraph on page 191 and 192 is missing a sentence. Create the missing sentence from the two sentences written above the paragraph. Use all the ideas but not necessarily all the words. Your new sentence should have an adjective clause and be a good supporting sentence. Write your new sentence on the lines in the paragraph.

Missing sentence ideas: This is the weather. + I like this weather the most.

How the Weather Affects Me

Some people do not believe that the weather can **affect** the way they feel, but it certainly affects me. On rainy days, I feel like watching a movie or staying in bed. Rainy weather makes me **lazy**. It makes me want to stay inside and take it easy. When the weather is bright and sunny, I feel energetic. This kind of weather makes me want to go outside. I want to play tennis or go to the beach. When the temperature is cool and the sun is shining, I feel like working. I feel **productive**. _____

_____

_____

As you can see, my mood is definitely **influenced** by the weather.

to affect: to change in some way

lazy: not active

productive: able to get things done

to influence: to have an effect on

191

Missing sentence ideas: Another word is *its*. + This word causes spelling problems.

Example Paragraph 63

Some English Spelling Problems

Some English words are difficult to spell. One word that many people misspell is *receive*. *Receive* is a problem because some people write the *i* before the *e*: *recieve*. The correct spelling is *receive* with the *e* before the *i*.

_____

_____

Some people **confuse** its with *it's*. In addition, some people write the word *its* with an apostrophe: *its'*. However, this last example is not an English word. Another example of bad spelling is **cemetery**. Some people change the last *e* to *a* because of the pronunciation: *cemetary*. These are just a few of the words that cause spelling problems for native and nonnative English speakers.

to confuse: to mix up in one's mind

a cemetery: a place where bodies are buried

ACTIVITY 7 Writing Original Sentences

Write a sentence that includes an adjective clause that describes each noun.

1. magazine

   I am reading a magazine that has many articles on fashion.

2. MP3 player

   Jennifer has an MP3 player that she listens to at the gym.

3. teacher

   _____

4. rhinoceros

   _____

5. towel

   _____

6. fountain

   _____

7. bat

_____

8. salary

_____

9. suitcase

_____

10. politician

_____

11. friend

_____

12. homework assignment

_____

Grammar for Writing

Using Modals to Add Meaning

Writers use **modals** to add extra information to the main verb in the sentence.

Common Modals

Modal	Meaning	Example Sentence: Subject + Modal + (*Not*) + Verb (Base Form)
should	to give advice	It is going to rain. You **should take** an umbrella.
must	to show necessity	You **must have** a visa to visit that country.
might	to show possibility	The weather is bad. We **might not go** to the beach.
can	to show ability	Roberto **can speak** three languages.

Follow these rules for sentences with modals:

- Do not use two modals together.

    ✗ We might can go to a new restaurant for dinner.

    ✓ We might go to a new restaurant for dinner.

- Do not use the word *to* between the modal and the verb.

    ✗ We might to play football tomorrow.

    ✓ We might play football tomorrow.

- To form the negative of *can,* use *cannot.*

    ✗ Yuri can not go to work because he is sick.

    ✓ Yuri cannot go to work because he is sick.

Answer the following questions about cooking a dinner for your friends. Use *should*, *must*, *might*, or *can*.

1. What should you do before your friends arrive at your house?

   _____

2. What must you do to the food before dinner?

   _____

3. What can your friends do to help with the dinner?

   _____

4. What might you cook if there are twenty guests?

   _____

5. What should you do if one of the guests has a food allergy?

   _____

Underline the modal that best completes each sentence. Sometimes both answers are correct. Be prepared to explain your answers.

Improve Your English More Quickly

Here is some good advice on how to improve your English more quickly. First, you (**1.** must / can) always speak English. This requirement (**2.** can / must) help improve your fluency. Second, you (**3.** should / might) also make friends with native speakers. Then you (**4.** can / must) talk to your new friends in English all the time. They (**5.** can / must) also correct your mistakes because they know the language well. Third, you (**6.** should / might) read a lot in English. This will improve your vocabulary. Finally, you (**7.** might / should) keep a daily journal. This (**8.** must / can) help your writing improve quickly. These suggestions (**9.** should / must) help your English get better more rapidly.

ACTIVITY 10 Original Writing

Imagine that a friend is coming to visit your country for two weeks. Your friend wants to know what to pack for his/her trip. Write a short letter giving advice on what to bring. Be sure to explain **why** these things are necessary. Use *should, must, might,* or *can.*

ACTIVITY 11 Editing: Error Correction and Sequencing

Correct the capitalization and punctuation mistakes in each sentence. Then put the sentences in the correct order (1 through 9) to make a good paragraph.

a. __1__ While victoria Falls, Iguazu falls, and niagara Falls all look different, they have several things in common.

b. _____ Additionally, Victoria Falls is on the border between zambia and zimbabwe.

c. _____ Visitors will find elaborate Bridges and viewing platforms on each side of all the waterfalls

d. _____ it is interesting to know how much these waterfalls have in common!

e. _____ For example, at least four major waterfalls come together to create iguazu Falls.

f. _____ Finally each waterfall is a major tourist attraction and the countries compete with each other to get the most tourists.

g. _____ next each large waterfall is made up of smaller waterfalls

h. _____ Iguazu Falls belongs to both brazil and argentina, and Niagara Falls is shared by canada and The United states

i. _____ first each waterfall is owned by two countries

Copy the sentences from Activity 11 in correct paragraph form. Be sure to add a title.

Example Paragraph 65

The paragraph is missing three sentences. The parts of the missing sentences are listed below. Unscramble the words to make correct sentences. Use the correct verb tense. Then write the complete sentences on the lines. Use correct capitalization and punctuation.

1. attend / in Istanbul, Turkey / Daniel / an important company meeting / in two days

2. his flight / at 5:00 P.M. / leave / from Gate 32

3. his suitcase / Daniel / put / in ten minutes / in the car

Example Paragraph 66

A Long Flight

1 _____

_____

_____

However, Daniel lives in Bogotá, Colombia, so he must catch a flight to Turkey before the meeting. Daniel is going to go to the airport today.

2 _____

_____

Because Daniel is going to take an international flight, he must be at the airport at 3:00 P.M. If he does not leave his house by noon, he is going to be late. It is almost 11:30 now. 3 _____

_____

_____

Then he will leave on his long trip.

ACTIVITY 14 Review: Identifying Sentence vs. Fragment

Identify each group of words as a fragment (*F*) or a complete sentence (*S*).

1. ___F___ Every year go to the beach in Hawaii.

2. ___S___ Kevin has an appointment with a chiropractor at 4:30 P.M.

3. _____ We are going to have a big party to celebrate Mark's next birthday.

4. _____ Ten years to become a medical doctor in the United States.

5. _____ Next Tuesday am going to see the new action movie.

6. _____ I got a nice gift for my birthday last week.

7. _____ Jenna is eating lunch and talking to her friends in the cafeteria right now.

8. _____ Because Meera works hard every day.

9. _____ That are Spanish-speaking countries in South America.

10. _____ Brett left his wallet at his friend's house last night.

ACTIVITY 15 Review: Identifying Sentence Types

Identify each sentence as a simple (*S*), compound (*CD*), or complex (*CX*) sentence. Add any missing commas as needed.

1. __CX__ The horse is an animal that is part of the *equidae* family.

2. _____ Zebras donkeys and okapis are all animals that look like the horse.

3. _____ Zebras look like small horses and they have black and white stripes.

4. _____ However, the zebra is a different species of animal.

5. _____ Donkeys look like small fuzzy horses that have long ears and black white or gray hair.

6. _____ Donkeys are definitely part of the *equus* family but they are also a different species from horses.

7. _____ An okapi's legs are striped black and white like a zebra's but its body is dark brown.

8. _____ Okapis are actually most closely related to giraffes.

9. _____ Some people may think that horses and ponies are separate species of animals because of their very different appearances.

10. _____ However, ponies are just small horses.

Editing: Grammar and Sentence Review

Correct the paragraph. There are 10 mistakes.

1 adjective clause mistake   2 comma mistakes   1 compound sentence mistake
2 capitalization mistakes   1 article mistake   1 possessive adjective mistake
1 mistake with word order   1 fragment

Example Paragraph 67

Visiting a New Country

Many reasons to visit a new country. First, you can see beautiful interesting and distant places. For example, you can visit a Kremlin and Red Square in moscow. Another reason to travel is to eat new types of food. If you visit Thailand, you can drink jasmine tea, you can eat coconut-flavored rice. Finally, you can meet new people which live in these exotic countries. you can talk to people and learn more about his likes and dislikes. As you can see, traveling to another country is important for reasons different.

Building Better Sentences: For further practice with the sentences and paragraphs in this unit, go to Practice 7 on page 257 in Appendix 1.

Building Better Vocabulary

ACTIVITY 17 **Word Associations**

Circle the word or phrase that is most closely related to the word or phrase on the left. If necessary, use a dictionary to check the meaning of words you do not know.

	A	B
1. a suitcase	a thing for holding clothes	a thing for holding money
2. to receive	to get something	to give something
3. evening	afternoon	night
4. a salary	money earned	money spent
5. to improve	to become better	to become worse
6. a flight	a ride in an airplane	a ride on a ship

7. exotic	the same and ordinary	strange and different
8. a journal*	a type of speaking	a type of writing
9. distant	far away	very close
10. a district	an area	a government

*Words that are part of the Academic Word List. See pages 245–246 for a complete list.

ACTIVITY 18 **Using Collocations**

Fill in each blank with the word that most naturally completes the phrase on the right. If necessary, use a dictionary to check the meaning of words you do not know.

1. dictionary / salary   a low _____

2. bright / few   a _____ light

3. hard / hardly   to work _____

4. for / with   to agree _____ someone

5. in / on   to go _____ strike

6. affect / effect   one _____ of the rain

7. make / tell   to _____ a suggestion

8. return /take   to _____ a flight

9. phrases / problems   to cause _____

10. in / on   to have something _____ common

ACTIVITY 19 Parts of Speech

Study the word forms. Fill in each blank with the best word form provided. Use the correct form of the verb. If necessary, use a dictionary to check the meaning of words you do not know. (NOTE: The word in bold is the original word that appears in the unit.)

Noun	Verb	Adjective	Sentence Practice
assignment	assign	Ø	1. Today's _____ is easy.
			2. My professor _____ too much homework last night.
energy	energ**ize**	**energetic**	3. Ellen's son is very _____.
			4. He has a lot of _____.
pronunciation	pronounce	Ø	5. Can you _____ the word *psychology*?
			6. Alex's _____ needs work.
confu**sion**	**confuse**	confus**ed**/confus**ing**	7. There was a lot of _____ at the concert.
			8. The directions on the test were _____.
attraction	attract	attract**ive**	9. The Empire State Building is a famous tourist _____ in New York City.
			10. Bright colors _____ attention.

Noun endings: *-ment, -tion, -sion, -ion*

Verb ending: *-ize*

Adjective endings: *-etic, -ed, -ing, -ive*

Original Student Writing

ACTIVITY 20 Original Writing Practice

In your opinion, which is better—cooking and eating food at home or eating out in a restaurant? Write a paragraph in which you answer this question and tell why.

Follow these steps for writing. Put a check (✓) next to each step as you complete it. When you finish your paragraph, use the checklist on page 204 to edit your work.

_____ STEP 1: In your first sentence, tell which dining choice you prefer.

_____ STEP 2: In the supporting sentences, give two or three reasons why you prefer this type of food.

_____ STEP 3: Give details for each reason you give.

_____ STEP 4: In the last sentence, summarize your opinion about the type of food that you prefer.

_____ STEP 5: Use at least one adjective clause.

_____ STEP 6: Use one or two modals.

_____ STEP 7: Use at least two of the vocabulary words or phrases presented in Activity 17, Activity 18, and Activity 19. Underline these words and phrases in your paragraph.

_____ STEP 8: Try to use time words and place phrases in some of the sentences in STEPS 2 or 3.

_____ STEP 9: Write at least one compound sentence in STEPS 2 or 3.

If you need ideas for words and phrases, see the Useful Vocabulary for Better Writing on pages 247–249.

☑ Checklist

1. ❑ I used the simple present tense in my paragraph.

2. ❑ I used articles correctly.

3. ❑ I used correct punctuation, including correct commas in compound and complex sentences.

4. ❑ I checked that each sentence has a subject and a verb—there are no fragments!

5. ❑ I gave my paragraph a title.

ACTIVITY 21 **Peer Editing**

Exchange papers from Activity 20 with a partner. Read your partner's paragraph. Then use Peer Editing Sheet 7 on NGL.Cengage.com/GW1 to help you comment on your partner's paragraph. Be sure to offer positive suggestions and comments that will help your partner improve his or her writing. Consider your partner's comments as you revise your own paragraph.

Additional Topics for Writing

Here are ten ideas for journal writing. Choose one or more of them to write about. Follow your teacher's directions. (We recommend that you skip a line after each line that you write. This gives your teacher a place to write comments.)

**PHOTO
TOPIC:** Look at the photo on pages 180–181. Write about an animal that you like. Describe the animal, tell where the animal lives, and tell why you like this animal so much.

TOPIC 2: Write about your dream house or apartment. Describe what this house looks like (how many rooms, what type of architecture, etc.). Write about the location of the house (in the mountains? on the beach? in a big city?).

TOPIC 3: Organized sports in school help children grow up to become better adults. Do you agree or disagree with this statement? Why?

TOPIC 4: Do you think that young children who know something about computers have an advantage in school today? Why or why not?

TOPIC 5: What is the worst decision that you have ever made? Give details about why it was a bad decision.

TOPIC 6: What is the best decision that you have ever made? Why was it a good decision? Did you come to this decision by yourself? How did you feel after you made this decision?

TOPIC 7: Write about a book that you like. Describe the book, briefly tell what happens in the story, and explain why you like this book.

TOPIC 8: Describe a painting that you like. Who painted it? What is in the painting? Describe the colors. What do you feel when you look at the painting?

TOPIC 9: Describe your favorite kind of shopping. Where do you shop? What do you shop for? What do you like about the experience?

TOPIC 10: Describe your favorite place to visit. Where is this place? When do you go there? Why do you go there?

Timed Writing

How quickly can you write in English? There are many times when you must write quickly, such as on a test. It is important to feel comfortable during those times. Timed-writing practice can make you feel better about writing quickly in English.

1. Take out a piece of paper.

2. Read the writing prompt below.

3. Brainstorm ideas for five minutes.

4. Write eight to ten sentences.

5. You have 20 minutes to write.

Describe something that is important to you. It can be a person, place, thing, or idea. Why is it important to you? Give examples. Provide as many details as possible.

_____

_____

_____

_____

_____

_____

_____

_____

_____

_____

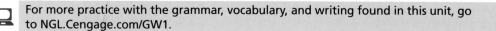 For more practice with the grammar, vocabulary, and writing found in this unit, go to NGL.Cengage.com/GW1.

Graffiti-covered cadillacs are stuck in the ground at the Cadillac Ranch in Amarillo, Texas.

Can you write your opinion on graffiti?

Review: Parts of a Paragraph

When you write a paragraph, there are several ideas to keep in mind.

Important Parts of a Paragraph

✓ A good paragraph has a **topic sentence** that states the main idea.

✓ All of the sentences in the paragraph are about **one topic**.

✓ The first line of a paragraph is **indented**.

✓ A good paragraph has a sufficient number of **supporting sentences**.

✓ The last sentence, or **concluding sentence**, brings the paragraph to a logical conclusion, and it often resembles the topic sentence.

ACTIVITY 1 Identifying Topic Sentences vs. Supporting Sentences

Each pair of sentences is about one topic. Identify which sentence is the topic sentence (*T*) and which is a supporting sentence (*S*). (Hint: The topic sentence gives more general information.)

1. **Topic: Kennedy Space Center**

   _____ **a.** You can take a tour of the rocket launch areas and experience a simulated shuttle launch.

   _____ **b.** Kennedy Space Center is an exciting place to visit.

2. Topic: The Definition of Patience

_____ **a.** A teacher often shows patience to young students at the end of the school day.

_____ **b.** Patience is the ability to continue doing something even if you do not see any results immediately.

3. Topic: The Golden Gate Bridge

_____ **a.** The Golden Gate Bridge is famous worldwide.

_____ **b.** The Golden Gate Bridge is 4200 feet (1280.2 m) long and rises 692 feet (211 m) above San Francisco Bay.

4. Topic: Making New Friends

_____ **a.** Some kids tried to be nice to me, but I did not want to talk to them.

_____ **b.** I learned the hard way how to make friends in a new school.

5. Topic: Cell Phones and Driving

_____ **a.** When drivers talk on cell phones, they become distracted and do not pay enough attention to driving.

_____ **b.** One of the recent developments of modern technology—cell phones—can be a danger to safe driving.

ACTIVITY 2 Ordering Sentences in a Paragraph

Put the sentences in a logical paragraph order. Then write the sentences in correct paragraph format on a separate piece of paper. Be sure to add an appropriate title.

_____ **a.** Instead, breakfast for them often consists of eggs with toast and coffee.

_____ **b.** People in Malaysia eat rice for breakfast, too, but their rice is cooked in coconut milk.

_____ **c.** Breakfast foods vary from country to country.

_____ **d.** However, people in most countries in Central and South America do not eat rice for breakfast.

_____ **e.** People eat this sweet, flavored rice with a red paste that is made of ground chili peppers and other ingredients.

_____ **f.** In Japan, for example, it is common to eat rice, soup, and fish for breakfast.

_____ **g.** From these varied breakfast items, it is clear that breakfast foods are different around the world.

ACTIVITY 3 Writing Concluding Sentences

Choose three topic sentences from Activity 1. Write a concluding sentence for each one.

1. _____

   _____

2. _____

   _____

3. _____

   _____

ACTIVITY 4 Choosing the Correct Verb Tense

Underline the correct verbs. Then answer the questions.

Example Paragraph 68

An Important Invention

I (**1.** believe / believed) that the light bulb is one of the most important inventions of all time. In the past, people (**2.** used / are using) candles to see at night. This light was very weak and difficult to see with. However, the light bulb now (**3.** allowed / allows) us to see things easily in the dark. This invention also (**4.** help / helps) us to do more work in one day. Before the light bulb, most work (**5.** ends / ended) at sundown. Now people can continue to work outdoors or in their offices for much longer at night. In addition, people can do more fun things

when it is dark. For example, sports fans (**6.** watch / watched) games at night on lighted fields, and music lovers (**7.** listen / are listening) to concerts in lighted stadiums. Without this incredible invention, people today would not have as many choices for work or play.

Post-Reading

1. What is the topic sentence of the paragraph? _____
_____

2. How many sentences does the paragraph have? _____

3. What reasons does the writer give to support the main idea? _____
_____
_____

4. What two verb tenses does the writer use? Why? _____
_____

5. What ideas/words do the topic sentence and concluding sentence share?
_____

ACTIVITY 5 **Original Writing Practice with Verb Tenses**

What do you think is an important invention in history? Write a short paragraph about it.

- Use the paragraph in Activity 4 as a model.
- Include a topic sentence.
- Include three examples to support your opinion.
- Give your paragraph a title.

_____

_____
_____
_____
_____
_____
_____
_____
_____
_____

Underline the correct verbs. Then answer the questions.

Example Paragraph 69

A Busy Day

Tomorrow (**1.** is / is going to be) a busy day for me. Usually, I (**2.** get / am getting) up at seven o' clock in the morning. However, tomorrow I (**3.** get / am going to get) up at five o'clock because I am going to go to the gym. After I finish at the gym, I (**4.** go / am going to go) to work. I usually (**5.** start / am starting) work at nine o'clock. Tomorrow I (**6.** start / am going to start) work at eight o'clock. After work, I frequently (**7.** have / am having) dinner with my friends. However, tomorrow I (**8.** go / am going to go) directly to my mother's house because it is her birthday. We (**9.** have / are going to have) a big party for her. I know it will be a full but fun day for me.

Post-Reading

1. What is the topic sentence of the paragraph? _____
   _____

2. How many sentences does the paragraph have? _____

3. What reasons does the writer give to support the main idea? _____
   _____
   _____

4. What two tenses does the writer use? Why? _____
   _____

5. What ideas/words do the topic sentence and concluding sentence share?
   _____

ACTIVITY 7 Editing for Subjects and Verbs

1. Reread your paragraph in Activity 5.
2. Circle all your subjects, and underline all your verbs. Be sure they agree in number.
3. Check that you used the correct verb tense.
4. Rewrite any sentences that need correction on the lines on page 213.
5. Ask a partner to check your writing.

_____

_____

_____

_____

_____

ACTIVITY 8 **Using Articles**

Underline the correct article. (NOTE: Ø means "no article.")

Example Paragraph 70

Underwater Adventure

I will never forget my first **encounter** with (**1.** a / an / Ø) shark. I was nineteen, and I was visiting Australia with my family. My father and I went scuba **diving** on (**2.** a / the / Ø) Great Barrier Reef. We went out to (**3.** a / the / Ø) reef with many other tourists on (**4.** a / an / the) special boat. When we got to (**5.** a / the / Ø) reef, the scuba diving

an encounter: a time when you meet someone or something

to dive: to jump into something

instructor helped us put on our equipment. Then we dove into
(**6.** a / the / Ø) clear blue water. Everything was so beautiful! There
were colorful fish and many different kinds of coral. I swam everywhere.
Suddenly, I saw (**7.** a / an / the) huge gray shark swim towards me.
I looked around for my father, but I was far away from him and
(**8.** a / an / the) group of tourists. What could I do? (**9.** A / An / The)
shark got closer and closer. I was so scared that I could not move. Just
when I thought that it might bite me, (**10.** a / an / the) shark turned
and swam (**11.** a / the / Ø) other way. Unbelievable! I quickly found my
father. Now I never swim off by myself when I go scuba diving.

ACTIVITY 9 **Editing for Articles**

1. Reread your paragraph in Activity 5.
2. Choose three sentences from your paragraph that contain articles. Write them below.
3. Ask a partner to check your sentences. Did you use the articles correctly?

_____

_____

_____

_____

_____

_____

Combine each underlined pair of sentences using the connectors *and, but,* or *so*. Remember to add a comma before the connecting word. You may have to delete some words. Then rewrite the sentences on the lines.

My First Car

My first car was the best car in the world. It was a Mustang. <u>My Mustang was bright blue. It was very powerful.</u> ① All my friends were **jealous** when they saw it. ② <u>They wanted to drive it. I told them they could not.</u> I said that they could be **passengers** or **pedestrians**. ③ <u>My friends did not want to walk. They always chose to be passengers.</u> However, the best thing about my car was the way it made me feel. ④ <u>Every weekend, I drove to the movie theater in that car. Every weekend, my friends rode with me.</u> We felt like movie stars because everyone **stared** at us in my beautiful blue car. I will never forget the fun that I had in that cool car.

jealous: feeling angry or unhappy because you wish you had something that someone else has

a passenger: a person who rides in any type of transportation

a pedestrian: a person who walks

to stare: to look at someone or something for a long time

1. _____

_____

2. _____

_____

3. _____

_____

4. _____

_____

ACTIVITY 11 Editing for Connectors

1. Reread your paragraph in Activity 5. Did you use any connectors?
2. If so, copy those sentences below.
3. If not, combine two of your sentences using a connector (*and, but, so*). Write your new sentence below.
4. Ask a partner to check your sentences. Did you use the connectors correctly?

_____

_____

_____

_____

_____

_____

ACTIVITY 12 Practicing Adjective Clauses with *Who* and *That*

Underline the correct word. Circle the two unrelated sentences.

Example Paragraph 72

How the Months of the Year Got Their Names

The names of all twelve months come from Roman culture and myths. First, there are several months (**1.** that / who) are named after Roman gods and goddesses. The Roman god of beginnings (**2.** that / who) gave us the month of January is Janus. The month (**3.** that / who) got its name from the Roman god of war is March. May and June **honor** the Roman goddesses Maia and Juno. Some months get their names from festivals. Both February and April come from special celebrations (**4.** that / who) **appeared** on the old Roman calendar. February usually only has 28 days. Two months (**5.** that / who) come in the summer got their names from Roman emperors. July is the month (**6.** that / who) honors Julius Caesar, and August is named for Emperor Augustus. These months are usually hot. Finally, September, October, November, and December are named after the seventh, eighth, ninth, and tenth months of the Roman calendar. The month names (**7.** that / who) are so commonly used today certainly have a very rich history.

to honor: to show respect and admiration for someone or something

to appear: to start to be seen

ACTIVITY 13 Editing for Adjective Clauses

1. Reread your paragraph in Activity 5. Did you use adjective clauses in your writing?
2. If so, copy those sentences below.
3. If not, combine two of your sentences using an adjective clause. Write your new sentence below.
4. Ask a partner to check your sentences. Did you use the adjective clauses correctly?

_____

_____

_____

_____

Writer's Note

Making Your Writing More Interesting

Remember to use a variety of sentence types (simple, compound, complex) in your writing. Different kinds of sentences will make your writing more interesting. You can also use adverbs and adjectives to add information and interest to your writing.

Combine all of the changes that you made to your original paragraph from Activity 5. Write your final version of the paragraph on the most important invention in history below.

_____

_____

_____

_____

_____

_____

_____

_____

_____

_____

_____

_____

Brief Reader Response: Writing a Response to Topics in the News

In academic classes, teachers frequently ask students to give their opinions about readings, pictures, movies, and other topics, such as current events in the news.

Verbs That Express an Opinion

When you write about your beliefs on a subject, you are giving your opinion. Use the words and phrases below when you write about your opinion.

Common Opinion Verbs	
Verbs	**Examples**
believe	I **believe** that no one should smoke in public.
feel	I **feel** that smoking is a personal decision.
think	I **think** that smoking is bad for one's health.
agree	I **agree** with the new laws that prohibit smoking.
disagree	I **disagree** with the new laws that prohibit smoking.
have mixed feelings	I **have mixed feelings** about smoking in public places. (This means the writer has more than one opinion on the topic, and the opinions conflict with each other.)

Read the paragraph. Then read the opinions that follow and answer the questions.

Smoking in Public Places

In the last two decades, many U.S. cities voted to **ban** smoking in public areas. The main reason for doing this was public health. The action was **controversial** because smokers felt **discriminated against**. Some **activists** believe that **prohibiting** smoking in public **establishments** is not the only solution to the problem. In fact, they suggest making separate areas for smokers and nonsmokers, **installing** advanced **ventilation systems**, and using other measures. However, the decision to ban smoking in public places is now a law.

to ban: to not allow; to make illegal

controversial: causing conflict or debate

to discriminate against: to judge or act upon unfairly

an activist: a person who works to support a political cause

to prohibit: not permit or allow

an establishment: a business

to install: to put a piece of machinery in place

a ventilation system: a machine that brings fresh air into a building

Opinion 1

Megan:

Because **secondhand smoke** causes cancer, I believe that banning smoking in public places is correct. If smoking is not permitted in government buildings like the post office or courthouse, why should any other public place be different? One day, smoking is going to be against the law, so this is not going to be an issue anymore. Until then, smokers should not create an unhealthy environment for people in public places.

secondhand smoke: the smoke created by a smoker that nearby nonsmokers breathe in

Post-Reading

1. What is the topic sentence of Megan's paragraph? _____

   _____

   _____

2. In your own words, write one sentence about how Megan feels about this issue.

   _____

   _____

3. List one argument that Megan uses to support her opinion. _____

Opinion 2

Scott:

I am not a smoker, but I disagree with the new laws that prohibit smoking. I think it is unfair to **single out** smokers and make them feel unaccepted. People in public places like restaurants are allowed to eat as much greasy, unhealthy food as they want, which can cause a heart attack and other serious health problems. Overeating is just as unhealthy as smoking is, yet only the smokers are punished. Adults should be able to make their own decision about smoking. I think that fewer smokers will want to visit public places as much, and businesses will suffer because of this law.

to single out: to pay special negative attention to someone

Post-Reading

1. What is the topic sentence of Scott's paragraph? _____

_____

2. In your own words, write one sentence about how Scott feels about this issue.

_____

_____

3. List one argument that Scott uses to support his opinion. _____

_____

_____

Opinion 3

Amanda:

I have mixed feelings about this new law. On the one hand, I am glad that when I go into a restaurant, cigarette smoke does not ruin the smell and flavor of my food. In the past, some restaurants were so smoky that I had to leave because I could not enjoy my food. Now, that will not happen to me again. On the other hand, I believe that there can be a **compromise**. I go to places like zoos and airports that have special areas for smoking, and I have no problems there. Maybe the two groups can reach a compromise that will satisfy everyone.

a compromise: a decision that everyone can agree to

Post-Reading

1. What is the topic sentence of Amanda's paragraph? _____

_____

2. In your own words, write one sentence about how Amanda feels about this issue.

_____

_____

3. How is Amanda's opinion different from Megan's and Scott's? _____

_____

_____

Writer's Note

Using *Should* to Soften Your Tone

You can use the word ***should*** to soften your tone when you give your opinion.

Strong: People must not talk on their cell phones in their cars.

Strong: People have to stop talking on their cell phones in their cars.

Softer: People should not talk on their cell phones in their cars.

ACTIVITY 16 **Original Writing**

Write a paragraph that tells if you support or oppose the idea of banning smoking in public places.

- Indent your paragraph.
- Make sure that your first sentence (the topic sentence) states your opinion.
- Include good supporting sentences.
- Give your paragraph a title.

If you need ideas for words and phrases, see the Useful Vocabulary for Better Writing on pages 247–249.

Writer's Note

The Importance of Editing

Remember that it is very important to edit your writing. When you edit your writing, you find and correct your mistakes. You should also ask other people to edit your work. They may find mistakes that you missed.

There is more information on editing your writing on pages 242–243 in the *Brief Writer's Handbook*.

ACTIVITY 17 Peer Editing

Exchange books with a partner and look at Activity 16. Read your partner's paragraph. Then use Peer Editing Sheet 8 on NGL.Cengage.com/GW1 to help you comment on your partner's paragraph. Be sure to offer positive suggestions and comments that will help your partner improve his or her writing. Consider your partner's comments as you revise your own paragraph.

ACTIVITY 18 Responding to a Reading Passage

Read the paragraph. Then read the opinions that follow, and answer the questions.

Example Paragraph 74

Controversy in the City

Recently, the City of New York announced it would continue its fight against **obesity**. The city's Department of Health wants to limit the size of all sweetened drinks to sixteen **ounces**. The department believes

obesity: being extremely overweight

an ounce: equal to 30 ml

that controlling the size of these drinks will help residents control the calories they **consume** and that this will help them lose weight. This ban would affect all restaurants, movie theaters, and food carts in the city. However, the Department of Health does not control supermarkets or convenience stores, so these businesses could continue to sell larger-sized drinks. This announcement has caused a great deal of **controversy** in the city, and its **opponents** promise to defeat it.

to consume: to eat or drink

a controversy: a debate or a conflict

an opponent: a person who disagrees with someone and wants to try to change that person's opinion

Opinion 1

Jason:

    I am not sure about this proposed ban. I believe obesity is a major health problem that we need to do something about. Reducing the size of sugary drinks would be one small step toward fighting obesity. However, I also think that local food cart owners will be the real losers. These small businesses do not offer free refills, and they will lose much needed money to convenience stores and restaurants where consumers can drink as much as they want for one price. Should these businesses possibly fail because America is fat?

Post-Reading

1. What is the topic sentence of Jason's paragraph? _____

_____

2. In your own words, write one sentence about how Jason feels about this case.

_____

_____

3. List one argument that Jason uses to support his idea. _____

_____

Opinion 2

Rebecca:

    I believe that the government's proposed ban is **ridiculous**. All adults have the right to choose how much they will or will not drink. If a person wants to have 32 ounces of a sugary drink, that person will find a way to get it. Many restaurants and theaters already have free refills, so it doesn't matter what the cup size is. Customers will just need to fill their glasses more. Even if the business does not have free refills, a person can choose to buy more than one drink at a time. It is simply too easy to get around this proposed rule. This is just another example of unnecessary governmental control.

ridiculous: unreasonable or foolish

Post-Reading

1. What is the topic sentence of Rebecca's paragraph? _____

_____

2. In your own words, write one sentence about how Rebecca feels about this case. _____

_____

_____

3. List one argument that Rebecca uses to support her idea. _____

_____

> ## Writer's Note
>
> ### Varying Your Vocabulary
>
> Vocabulary is a key part of good writing. Your level of vocabulary shows your English proficiency. The reader's opinion of your writing will be higher if you use better vocabulary.
>
> Like using sentence variety, varying your vocabulary will make your writing more interesting. Follow these guidelines:
>
> - Use synonyms, phrases, and sometimes whole sentences to say the information a different way.
> - Avoid repeating the same words too many times in a row.
> - Use pronouns as appropriate.

Building Better Vocabulary

ACTIVITY 19 Word Associations

Circle the word or phrase that is most closely related to the word or phrase on the left. If necessary, use a dictionary to check the meaning of words you do not know.

	A	B
1. a compromise	an agreement	a disagreement
2. an invention	a mountain	a telephone
3. a pedestrian	a rider	a walker
4. a decision	an action	a feeling
5. a customer	a consumer	an entrepreneur
6. banned	can do something	cannot do something

	A	B
7. controversial*	people agree	people disagree
8. to prohibit*	to allow	to ban
9. recently	in the near future	in the near past
10. an encounter*	a meeting	an understanding

*Words that are part of the Academic Word List. See pages 245–246 for a complete list.

ACTIVITY 20 Using Collocations

Fill in each blank with the word that most naturally completes the phrase on the right. If necessary, use a dictionary to check the meaning of words you do not know.

1. at / on to stare _____ something

2. get / put to _____ the food in the refrigerator

3. allow / classify to not _____ smoking in public

4. decision / solution to make a _____ about something

5. about / against to discriminate _____ a person

6. about / for to vote _____ a candidate

7. give / have to _____ mixed feelings

8. make / reach to _____ a compromise

9. against / from to be banned _____ doing something

10. passengers / pedestrians _____ on a train

ACTIVITY 21 Parts of Speech

Study the word forms. Fill in each blank with the best word form provided. Use the correct form of the word. If necessary, use a dictionary to check the meaning of words you do not know. (NOTE: The word in bold is the original word that appears in the unit.)

Noun	Verb	Adjective	Sentence Practice
controversy		controvers<u>ial</u>	**1.** New York City's ban on sugary drinks is _____.
			2. I like _____. It makes things exciting.
swimm<u>ers</u> / swimm<u>ing</u> (PEOPLE) / (A THING)	**swim**	Ø	**3.** _____ is an Olympic sport.
			4. _____ have muscular bodies.

(Continued)

Noun	Verb	Adjective	Sentence Practice
difference	differ	**different**	**5.** The twins _____ in their political views.
			6. There are _____ between British English and American English.
power	∅	**powerful**	**7.** My car's engine has the _____ to drive up the mountain.
			8. Al gave a _____ speech.
disagreement	**disagree**	disagreeable	**9.** There was a _____ between the coach and his players.
			10. Many people _____ about the correct way to load a dishwasher.

Noun endings: *-er, -ing, -ence, -ment*

Adjective endings: *-al, -ent, -ful, -able*

Original Student Writing

ACTIVITY 22 Original Writing

Reread Example Paragraph 74 in Activity 18. Then reread the two opinions and review your answers. Write a paragraph that states your opinion about this case. Tell if you agree or disagree with what the City of New York plans to do. Follow these instructions:

- Make sure that the first sentence you write (topic sentence) states the opinion you agree with.

- Include good supporting sentences.

- Include a concluding sentence.

- Give your paragraph a title.

- Use at least two of the vocabulary words or phrases presented in Activity 19, Activity 20, and Activity 21. Underline these words and phrases in your paragraph.

If you need ideas for words and phrases, see the Useful Vocabulary for Better Writing on pages 247–249.

_____

_____

_____

_____

_____

_____

_____

_____

_____

_____

_____

_____

ACTIVITY 23 **Peer Editing**

Exchange books with a partner and look at Activity 22. Read your partner's paragraph. Then use Peer Editing Sheet 9 on NGL.Cengage.com/GW1 to help you comment on your partner's paragraph. Be sure to offer positive suggestions and comments that will help your partner improve his or her writing. Consider your partner's comments as you revise your own paragraph.

Additional Topics for Writing

Here are ten ideas for journal writing. Choose one or more of them to write about. Follow your teacher's directions. (We recommend that you skip a line after each line that you write. This gives your teacher a place to write comments.)

PHOTO
TOPIC: Look at the photo on pages 206–207. Some people believe that graffiti in public places is a form of art. Others believe that it is vandalism. What is your opinion on graffiti?

TOPIC 2: Do you think that crying is a sign of strength or a sign of weakness? Why?

TOPIC 3: Some schools require students to wear uniforms. Do you agree or disagree? Explain.

TOPIC 4: When someone does something very wrong, should they be given a second chance? Give an example to explain your feelings about this.

TOPIC 5: At what age should children be allowed to have their own phones? Should parents be allowed to read their children's text messages and listen to their voice mail? Explain.

TOPIC 6: Should women be allowed to serve in combat positions in the military? Why or why not?

TOPIC 7: The governments of some countries require entertainers (for example Lady Gaga and Katie Perry) to change parts of their acts before they can perform in their countries. Should the entertainers change their acts, or should they refuse to perform there? Explain.

TOPIC 8: Localvores are people who believe it is good to eat only food that is grown very close to where they live. They believe this helps the environment and local farmers. How do you feel about this idea? Do you believe you could successfully be a localvore? Why or why not?

TOPIC 9: In the United States, music CDs that contain explicit lyrics receive a warning sticker. Do you believe that it is necessary for music to have this type of label? Explain why you feel this way.

TOPIC 10: Think of a situation that is currently affecting your school, community, or city. Why do people disagree about this situation? What is your opinion? Is there a good solution?

For more practice with the grammar, vocabulary, and writing found in this unit, go to NGL.Cengage.com/GW1.

Brief Writer's Handbook

Definitions of Useful Language Terms

Adjective
An adjective is a word that describes a noun.

Lexi is a very **smart** girl.

Adverb
An adverb is a word that describes a verb, an adjective, or another adverb.

The secretary types **quickly**. She types **very quickly**.

Article
The definite article is *the*. The indefinite articles are *a* and *an*.

The teacher gave **an** assignment to **the** students.
Jillian is eating **a** banana.

Clause
A clause is a group of words that has a subject-verb combination. Sentences can have one or more clauses.

subj.   verb
Roger attends the College of New Jersey.
clause

subj.   verb   subj. verb
Christopher needs to write his report because **he   wants** to pass the class.
clause 1   clause 2

Noun
A noun is a person, place, thing, or idea.

Sandra likes to eat **sandwiches** for lunch.
Love is a very strong **emotion**.

Object
An object is a word that comes after a transitive verb or a preposition.

Jim bought a new **car**.
I left my **jacket** in the **house**.

Predicate
A predicate is the part of a sentence that shows what a subject does.

subject   predicate
Mr. Johnston walked to the park.

subject   predicate
My neighbor's cat was digging a hole in the yard.

Preposition
A preposition is a word that can show location, time, and direction. Some common prepositions are *around, at, behind, between, from, on, in, near, to, over, under,* and *with*. Prepositions can also consist of two words (*next to*) or three words (*in addition to*).

Punctuation
Punctuation includes the period (.), comma (,), question mark (?), and exclamation point (!).

Subject
The subject of a sentence tells who or what the sentence is about.

My science teacher gave us a homework assignment. **It** was difficult.

Tense
A verb has tense. Tense shows when the action happened.

Simple Present: She **walks** to school every day.
Present Progressive: She **is walking** to school now.
Simple Past: She **walked** to school yesterday.
Past Progressive: She **was walking** to school when she saw her friend.
Simple Future: She **is going to walk** to school tomorrow.
Simple Future: She **will walk** to school tomorrow.

Verb	A verb is a word that shows the action of a sentence.

They **speak** French.

My father **works** at the power plant.

Review of Verb Tenses

Verb Tense	Affirmative	Negative	Usage
Simple Present	I work you take he studies she does we play they have	I do not work you do not take he does not study she does not do we do not play they do not have	• for routines, habits, and other actions that happen regularly • for facts and general truths
Simple Past	I worked you took he studied she did we played they had	I did not work you did not take he did not study she did not do we did not play they did not have	• for actions that were completed in the past
Present Progressive	I am working you are taking he is studying she is doing we are playing they are having*	I am not working you are not taking he is not studying she is not doing we are not playing they are not having*	• for actions that are happening now • for future actions if a future time adverb is used or understood
Simple Future (*Be Going To*)	I am going to work you are going to take he is going to study she is going to do we are going to play they are going to have	I am not going to work you are not going to take he is not going to study she is not going to do we are not going to play they are not going to have	• for plans that are already made • for predictions based on an action happening in the present
Simple Future (*Will*)	I will work you will take he will study she will do we will play they will have	I will not work you will not take he will not study she will not do we will not play they will not have	• for future plans or decisions that are made at the moment of speaking • for strong predictions • for promises/offers to help
Present Perfect	I have worked you have taken he has studied she has done we have played they have had	I have not worked you have not taken he has not studied she has not done we have not played they have not had	• for actions that began in the past and continue until the present • for actions in the indefinite past time • for repeated actions in the past
Past Progressive	I was working you were taking he was studying she was doing we were playing they were having*	I was not working you were not taking he was not studying she was not doing we were not playing they were not having*	• for longer actions in the past that are interrupted by other actions or events

Have can be used in progressive tenses only when it has an active meaning in special expressions, such as:

- *have* a party
- *have* a good time
- *have* a bad time
- *have* a baby

4. If a verb/noun ends in a vowel + *y*, add –*s*. Do not change the *y*.

pay	pays
boy	boys
destroy	destroys

5. Add –*es* to *go* and *do*.

go	goes
do	does

Spelling Rules for Regular Simple Past Tense Verbs

1. Add -*ed* to the base form of most verbs.

start	started
finish	finished
wash	washed

2. Add only -*d* when the base form ends in an *e*.

live	lived
care	cared
die	died

3. If a verb ends in a consonant + *y*, change the *y* to *i* and add -*ed*.

dry	dried
carry	carried
study	studied

4. If a verb ends in a vowel + *y,* do not change the *y*. Just add -*ed*.

play	played
stay	stayed
destroy	destroyed

5. If a verb has one syllable and ends in a consonant + vowel + consonant (CVC), double the final consonant and add -*ed*.

stop	sto**pp**ed
CVC	
rob	ro**bb**ed
CVC	

6. If a verb ends in a *w* or *x*, do not double the final consonant. Just add -*ed*.

sew	sewed
mix	mixed

7. If a verb that ends in CVC has two syllables and the <u>second</u> syllable is stressed, double the final consonant and add -*ed*.

ad mit'	admi**tt**ed
oc cur'	occu**rr**ed
per mit'	permi**tt**ed

8. If a verb that ends in CVC has two syllables and the <u>first</u> syllable is stressed, do *not* double the final consonant. Just add -*ed*.

hap' pen	happe**n**ed
lis' ten	liste**n**ed
o' pen	ope**n**ed

Irregular Simple Past Tense Verbs

These are some of the more common irregular verbs in English.

Base Form	Simple Past
be (am/is/are)	was/were
become	became
begin	began
bite	bit
bleed	bled
blow	blew
break	broke
bring	brought
build	built
buy	bought
catch	caught
choose	chose
come	came
cost	cost
cut	cut
do	did
draw	drew
drink	drank
drive	drove
eat	ate
fall	fell
feel	felt
fight	fought
find	found
flee	fled
forget	forgot
get	got
give	gave
grow	grew
have	had
hear	heard
hide	hid
hit	hit
hold	held

Base Form	Simple Past
hurt	hurt
keep	kept
know	knew
leave	left
let	let
lose	lost
make	made
pay	paid
put	put
read	read
run	ran
say	said
see	saw
sell	sold
send	sent
set	set
sing	sang
sink	sank
sit	sat
sleep	slept
speak	spoke
spend	spent
stand	stood
steal	stole
swim	swam
take	took
teach	taught
tell	told
think	thought
throw	threw
understand	understood
wear	wore
win	won
write	wrote

Spelling of the *-ing* (Present Participle) Form of Verbs

1. Add *-ing* to the base form of most verbs.

catch	catching
wear	wearing
go	going

2. If a verb ends in a consonant + *e*, drop the *e* and add *-ing.*

write	writing
drive	driving
take	taking

3. If a verb has one syllable and ends in a consonant + vowel + consonant (CVC), double the final consonant and add *-ing.*

run	ru**nn**ing
CVC	
sit	si**tt**ing
CVC	
stop	sto**pp**ing
CVC	

4. If a verb ends in a *w*, *x*, or *y*, do not double the final consonant. Just add *-ing.*

sew	sewing
mix	mixing
say	saying

5. If a verb that ends in CVC has two syllables and the <u>second</u> syllable is stressed, double the final consonant and add *-ing.*

be gin'	begi**nn**ing
ad mit'	admi**tt**ing
re fer'	refe**rr**ing

6. If a verb that ends in CVC has two syllables and the <u>first</u> syllable is stressed, do *not* double the final consonant. Just add *-ing.*

o' pen	ope**n**ing
lis' ten	liste**n**ing
hap' pen	happe**n**ing

Common Stative (Non-action) Verbs

Common Stative (Non-action) Verbs			
agree	hate	mean	seem
be	have	need	smell
believe	hear	own	taste
cost	know	prefer	think
dislike	like	remember	understand
forget	love	see	want

In general, stative verbs do not use the progressive tense because they do not show an action, so the *-ing* form is rarely used.

    ✗ She is drinking coffee because she is <u>disliking</u> green tea.
    ✓ She is drinking coffee because she dislikes green tea.

Spelling Exceptions for *A* and *An*

You must use *a* or *an* with a single count noun with a general meaning. Use *a* before word that starts with a consonant sound. Use *an* before a word that starts with a vowel sound. However, the letters *h* and *u* have exceptions.

Word Begins with H	When the *h* is pronounced, use *a*.	a horse a hat a hot day a huge dog
	When the *h* is silent, use *an*. (This is because the first sound in the word is a vowel sound.)	an hour an honor an honorable man an herbal tea
Word Begins with U	When the *u* sounds like "uh," use *an*.	an umpire an umbrella an ugly shirt an uncomfortable chair
	When the *u* sounds like "you," use *a*.	a university a uniform a useful invention a unique idea

Definite Article *The*

Use the article *the* when you are writing about a specific noun.

1. Use *the* for the second (and subsequent) time you write about something.

    I bought a new coat yesterday. **The** coat is blue and gray.

2. Use *the* when the speaker and listener both know about or are familiar with the subject.

    My brother called and said, "I'm locked out of **the house**."

3. Use *the* when the noun you are referring to is unique—there is only one. This thing can be natural or manmade.

    The Sun and **the** Earth are both in **the Milky Way Galaxy**.

    The Eiffel Tower is a beautiful monument.

    I am going to visit **the Sidney Opera House** next summer.

    The New Caledonia Barrier Reef is an important home for green sea turtles.

4. Use *the* with specific time periods.

    You must be very quiet for **the next hour**.

5. Use *the* when the other words in your sentence make the noun specific.

    The cat in the picture is very pretty. (*In the picture* specifies which cat you are talking about.)

6. Do not use *the* before names or when you talk about something in general.

    Mikhail Bulgakov is a famous Russian writer.

    Jason is going to make a table with **wood**.

7. Some geographic locations require *the*, but others do not. Cities, states, countries, continents, and lakes do not use *the*.

country name

Sylvie is from **Venezuela**. She lives near **Lake Maracaibo**.

lake name

However, if the location ends in *-s* (plural, such as a group of islands), or the words *united, union, kingdom*, or *republic* are in the name of the country, use *the*.

We are going to **the Bahamas** for our vacation. (The country name ends with *-s*.)

Who is the president of **the United States**? (*United* is in the country name.)

Most buildings, bodies of water (except lakes), mountain chains, and deserts use *the*.

building name

The White House is in Washington, DC.

river name

The Amazon is a very long river in South America.

(NO *THE*)
lake name

Lake Baikal is a large freshwater lake in Russia.

Common Non-count Nouns

Count nouns can be counted: *three* dogs, *two* computers, *one* house, *ten* tomatoes. A non-count noun cannot be counted.

Common Non-count Nouns	
Food items	butter, sugar, salt, pepper, soup, rice, fish, meat, flour, bread
Liquids	milk, coffee, water, juice, cream
Academic subjects	English, math, science, music, biology
Abstract ideas	love, honesty, poverty, crime, advice, luck, pain, hate, beauty, humor
Others	homework, information, money, furniture, traffic

Non-count nouns use quantifiers such as *much* and *a little*.

We do not have **much** time to finish the assignment.

I drank **a little** water this morning.

Count nouns use quantifiers such as *many* and *a few*.

There are **many** cars in the parking lot.

Dayna only has **a few** dollars in her wallet.

There is more information on quantifiers on page 240 in the *Brief Writer's Handbook*.

Possessive Pronouns

In general, possessive pronouns are used in spoken English. However, it is important to know how to use them. Possessive pronouns take the place of a possessive adjective + noun combination. In a sentence, a possessive pronoun can be a subject or an object.

Possessive Pronoun	Example
mine	That is not your book. It is **mine** (= my book).
yours (singular)	I don't have my pencil. I need to use **yours** (= your book).
his	My ring is silver, but **his** (= his ring) is gold.
hers	Carol has my cell phone, and I have **hers** (= her cell phone).
ours	Your room is on the first floor. **Ours** (= our room) is on the fifth floor.
yours (plural)	Our class got to have a special party. **Yours** (= your class) did not.
theirs	Jenny likes her class, and Karl and Jim like **theirs** (= their class), too.

Order of Adjectives

Adjectives can go before nouns. When more than one adjective is used before a noun, there is a certain order for the adjectives.

Example: He has a **brown** dog. It is an **enormous** dog.

✗ He has a brown enormous dog.

✓ He has an enormous brown dog.

In general, there are seven kinds of adjectives. They are used in this order:

1. size   *small, large, huge*

2. opinion   *beautiful, nice, ugly*

3. shape   *round, square, oval*

4. condition   *broken, damaged, burned*

5. age   *old, young, new*

6. color   *red, white, green*

7. origin   *French, American, Korean*

It is common to have two adjectives before a noun but rare to have three or more adjectives before a noun. When there is more than one adjective before a noun, follow the order above. The noun always goes last. Remember that this list is only a general guideline.

✗ a white Japanese small truck

✓ a small white Japanese truck

✗ a broken large dish

✓ a large broken dish

More Prepositions

Here are a few more common prepositions of location. Remember that a preposition is usually followed by a noun (or pronoun). In the chart, the preposition shows the location of the ball (in relation to the box).

Preposition	Example
in	The gift is **in** the box.
on	Marta's gift is **on** the table.
under	Pedro keeps his shoes **under** his bed.
above/over	Sheila held the umbrella **over** her head to stay dry.
between	The milk is **between** the eggs and the butter.
in front of	Mark was standing in **front of** the restaurant.
in back of/behind	My shirt fell **behind** my dresser.
across…from	There is a supermarket **across** the street **from** my house.
next to/beside	The mailman left the package **next to** the door.

Editing Your Writing

While you must be comfortable writing quickly, you also need to be comfortable with improving your work. Writing an assignment is not always a one-step process. It is often a multiple-step process. During your timed writings in Units 3–7, you probably made some changes to your work to make it better. However, you may not have fixed all of the errors. The paper that you turned in to your teacher is called a **first draft**, or **rough draft**.

A first draft can often be improved. One way to improve your writing is to ask a classmate, friend, or teacher to read it and make suggestions. Your reader may discover that your paragraph is missing a topic sentence or that there are grammar mistakes. Your partner may also not mark all the mistakes in your paper. You may not always like or agree with your reader's comments, but being open to suggestions will make you a better writer.

This section will help you become more familiar with how to identify and correct errors in your writing.

Step 1

Below is a student's first draft for a timed writing. The writing prompt for this assignment was "Write about a very happy or a very sad event in your life." As you read the first draft, look for areas that need improvement, and write your comments in the margin. For example, does every sentence have a subject and a verb? Does the writer always use the correct verb tense and the correct punctuation? Does the paragraph have a topic sentence?

My Saddest Day

The day I came for the U.S. is my saddest. That night my family gave me a big party. We staied up all night. In the morning, all the people were go to the airport. We cryed and said good-bye. they kissed and huged me. i think that i will not see them ever again. i was sad in united states for six months. now i feel better. that was my saddest day.

Step 2

Read the teacher comments on the first draft of "My Saddest Day." Are these the same things that you noticed?

My Saddest Day

Remember to indent

The day I came for the U.S. (is) my saddest. That night my family gave me a big party. We (staied)
was

up all night. In the morning, all the people (were go) to the airport. We (cryed) and said good-bye.
There is no "be" form with simple past

they kissed and (huged) me. i (think) that i will not see them ever again. i was sad in united states
Always put "the" in front of "United States"

for six months. now i feel better. that was my saddest day.

You have some good ideas in this paragraph. I really like your topic sentence and concluding sentence. However, you write about three different time frames. You write about the night you left your country, the day you arrived in the United States, and six months after you arrived. Choose one of these times and write about that. I'd really like to learn about your party.

Verbs: You must review the spelling rules for the simple past tense. You had a very hard time with this. Also, be careful with irregular forms. The incorrect forms distract from your ideas. I corrected your first mistake. Fix the others I've circled.

I underlined some capitalization errors. Please fix these, too.

Step 3

Now read the second draft of this paper. How is it the same as the first draft? How is it different? Did the writer fix all the sentence mistakes?

My Saddest Day

The night before I came for the U.S. was my saddest day. That night my family gave me a big party. All my family and friends were come to it. We sang, danced, and ate many food. We stayed up all night. We talked about my new life. When everyone left, we cried and said good-bye. They kissed and hugged me. I think I will not see them ever again. Finally, I went to bed at 4:00 in the morning. However, I could not sleep because I was so sad. I was sad in the United States for six months. Now I feel better, but that was my saddest day.

Connectors

Connectors in Compound Sentences

Connectors in compound sentences, or coordinating conjunctions, are used to connect two clauses (sentences). A comma usually appears before a connecting word that separates two clauses in a compound sentence.

Purpose	Coordinating Conjunction	Example
To show reason	for*	He ate a sandwich, **for** he was hungry.
To add information	and	Miki lives in Toronto, **and** she is a student.
To add negative information	nor**	Roberto does not like opera, **nor** does he enjoy hip-hop.
To show contrast	but†	The exam was difficult, **but** everyone passed.
To give a choice	or	We can eat Chinese food, **or** we can order a pizza.
To show concession/ contrast	yet†	There was a hurricane warning, **yet** many people went to the beach.
To show a result	so	It was raining, **so** we decided to stay home last night.

*The conjunction *for* is not common in English. It may be used in literary writing, but it is almost never used in spoken English.

**Notice that question word order is used in the clause that follows *nor*.

†The conjunctions *but* and *yet* have similar meanings. However, *yet* is generally used to show a stronger or unexpected contrast.

Many writers remember these conjunctions with the acronym *FANBOYS*. Each letter represents one conjunction:

$$F = for, A = and, N = nor, B = but, O = or, Y = yet, and S = so$$

Connectors in Complex Sentences

Connectors in complex sentences, or subordinating conjunctions, are used to connect a dependent clause and an independent clause. When the sentence begins with the dependent clause, a comma should be used after the clause.

Purpose	Subordinating Conjunction	Example
To show reason/cause	because since as	He ate a sandwich **because** he was hungry. **Since** he was hungry, he ate a sandwich. **As** he was hungry, he ate a sandwich.
To show contrast	although even though though while	**Although** the exam was difficult, everyone passed. **Even though** the exam was difficult, everyone passed. **Though** the exam was difficult, everyone passed. Deborah is a dentist **while** John is a doctor.
To show a time relationship	after before until while when as as soon as	**After** we ate dinner, we went to a movie. We ate dinner **before** we went to a movie. I will not call you **until** I finish studying. **While** the pasta is cooking, I will cut the vegetables. **When** Jennifer gets home, she is going to eat dinner. **As** I was leaving the office, it started to rain. **As soon as** class ended, Mia ran out the door.
To show condition	if even if	**If** it rains tomorrow, we will stay home. We are going to go to the park **even if** it rains tomorrow.

Academic Word List

Averil Coxhead (2000)

The following words are on the Academic Word List (AWL). The AWL is a list of the 570 highest-frequency academic word families that regularly appear in academic texts. The AWL was compiled by researcher Averil Coxhead based on her analysis of a 3.5 million word corpus.

abandon	available	confirm	detect	evolve
abstract	aware	conflict	deviate	exceed
academy	behalf	conform	device	exclude
access	benefit	consent	devote	exhibit
accommodate	bias	consequent	differentiate	expand
accompany	bond	considerable	dimension	expert
accumulate	brief	consist	diminish	explicit
accurate	bulk	constant	discrete	exploit
achieve	capable	constitute	discriminate	export
acknowledge	capacity	constrain	displace	expose
acquire	category	construct	display	external
adapt	cease	consult	dispose	extract
adequate	challenge	consume	distinct	facilitate
adjacent	channel	contact	distort	factor
adjust	chapter	contemporary	distribute	feature
administrate	chart	context	diverse	federal
adult	chemical	contract	document	fee
advocate	circumstance	contradict	domain	file
affect	cite	contrary	domestic	final
aggregate	civil	contrast	dominate	finance
aid	clarify	contribute	draft	finite
albeit	classic	controversy	drama	flexible
allocate	clause	convene	duration	fluctuate
alter	code	converse	dynamic	focus
alternative	coherent	convert	economy	format
ambiguous	coincide	convince	edit	formula
amend	collapse	cooperate	element	forthcoming
analogy	colleague	coordinate	eliminate	found
analyze	commence	core	emerge	foundation
annual	comment	corporate	emphasis	framework
anticipate	commission	correspond	empirical	function
apparent	commit	couple	enable	fund
append	commodity	create	encounter	fundamental
appreciate	communicate	credit	energy	furthermore
approach	community	criteria	enforce	gender
appropriate	compatible	crucial	enhance	generate
approximate	compensate	culture	enormous	generation
arbitrary	compile	currency	ensure	globe
area	complement	cycle	entity	goal
aspect	complex	data	environment	grade
assemble	component	debate	equate	grant
assess	compound	decade	equip	guarantee
assign	comprehensive	decline	equivalent	guideline
assist	comprise	deduce	erode	hence
assume	compute	define	error	hierarchy
assure	conceive	definite	establish	highlight
attach	concentrate	demonstrate	estate	hypothesis
attain	concept	denote	estimate	identical
attitude	conclude	deny	ethic	identify
attribute	concurrent	depress	ethnic	ideology
author	conduct	derive	evaluate	ignorant
authority	confer	design	eventual	illustrate
automate	confine	despite	evident	image

immigrate	liberal	parameter	reinforce	subsidy
impact	license	participate	reject	substitute
implement	likewise	partner	relax	successor
implicate	link	passive	release	sufficient
implicit	locate	perceive	relevant	sum
imply	logic	percent	reluctance	summary
impose	maintain	period	rely	supplement
incentive	major	persist	remove	survey
incidence	manipulate	perspective	require	survive
incline	manual	phase	research	suspend
income	margin	phenomenon	reside	sustain
incorporate	mature	philosophy	resolve	symbol
index	maximize	physical	resource	tape
indicate	mechanism	plus	respond	target
individual	media	policy	restore	task
induce	mediate	portion	restrain	team
inevitable	medical	pose	restrict	technical
infer	medium	positive	retain	technique
infrastructure	mental	potential	reveal	technology
inherent	method	practitioner	revenue	temporary
inhibit	migrate	precede	reverse	tense
initial	military	precise	revise	terminate
initiate	minimal	predict	revolution	text
injure	minimize	predominant	rigid	theme
innovate	minimum	preliminary	role	theory
input	ministry	presume	route	thereby
insert	minor	previous	scenario	thesis
insight	mode	primary	schedule	topic
inspect	modify	prime	scheme	trace
instance	monitor	principal	scope	tradition
institute	motive	principle	section	transfer
instruct	mutual	prior	sector	transform
integral	negate	priority	secure	transit
integrate	network	proceed	seek	transmit
integrity	neutral	process	select	transport
intelligent	nevertheless	professional	sequence	trend
intense	nonetheless	prohibit	series	trigger
interact	norm	project	sex	ultimate
intermediate	normal	promote	shift	undergo
internal	notion	proportion	significant	underlie
interpret	notwithstanding	prospect	similar	undertake
interval	nuclear	protocol	simulate	uniform
intervene	objective	psychology	site	unify
intrinsic	obtain	publication	so-called	unique
invest	obvious	publish	sole	utilize
investigate	occupy	purchase	somewhat	valid
invoke	occur	pursue	source	vary
involve	odd	qualitative	specific	vehicle
isolate	offset	quote	specify	version
issue	ongoing	radical	sphere	via
item	option	random	stable	violate
job	orient	range	statistic	virtual
journal	outcome	ratio	status	visible
justify	output	rational	straightforward	vision
label	overall	react	strategy	visual
labor	overlap	recover	stress	volume
layer	overseas	refine	structure	voluntary
lecture	panel	regime	style	welfare
legal	paradigm	region	submit	whereas
legislate	paragraph	register	subordinate	whereby
levy	parallel	regulate	subsequent	widespread

Useful Vocabulary for Better Writing

Try these useful words and phrases as you write your sentences and paragraphs. Many of these words and phrases are found in the *Great Writing 1: Great Sentences for Great Paragraphs* model paragraphs, and they can make your writing sound more academic, natural, and fluent.

Topic Sentences

Words and phrases	Examples
There are QUANTIFIER (ADJECTIVE) SUBJECT…	*There are* many good places to visit in my country.
SUBJECT *must follow* QUANTIFIER (ADJECTIVE) *steps to* VERB…	A tourist *must follow* several simple *steps to* get a visa to visit my country.
There are QUANTIFIER (ADJECTIVE) *types / methods / ways…*	*There are* three different *types* of runners.
It is ADJECTIVE *to* VERB…	*It is* easy *to* make ceviche.

Supporting Sentence Markers

Words and phrases	Examples
One NOUN…	*One* reason to visit my country is the wonderful weather.
Another NOUN… *… another* NOUN	*Another* reason to visit my country is the delicious food. The delicious food is *another* reason to visit my country.
The first / second / next / final NOUN…	*The final* reason to visit my country is its wonderful people.

Giving and Adding Examples

Words and phrases	Examples
For example, S + V. *For instance,* S + V.	My instructor gives us so much homework. *For example,* yesterday he gave us five pages of grammar work.

Concluding Sentences

Words and phrases	Examples
In conclusion, S + V.	*In conclusion,* I believe that my parents are the best in the world.
It is clear that S + V.	*It is clear that* Guatemala is the best tourist destination in South America.
If you follow these important steps in VERB + *-ING…,* S + V.	*If you follow these important steps in* fixing a computer, you will not need to call an expert.

Telling a Story

Words and phrases	Examples
When I was X, I would VERB…	*When I was* a teenager, *I would* go to the beach with my friends every day.
When I think about that time, S + V.	*When I think about that time*, I remember my grandparents' love for me.
I will never forget NOUN…	*I will never forget* the day I left my country.
I can still remember NOUN… *I will always remember* NOUN…	*I can still remember* the day I started my first job.
X *was the best / worst day of my life.*	My sixteenth birthday *was the best day of my life.*
Every time S +V, S + V.	*Every time* I tried to speak English, my tongue refused to work!

Describing a Process

Words and phrases	Examples
First (*Second, Third*, etc.), *Next*, … / *After that*, … / *Then* … *Finally*, …	*First*, you cut the fish and vegetables into small pieces. *Next*, you add the lime juice. *After that*, you add in the seasonings. *Finally*, you mix everything together well.
The first thing you should do is VERB…	*The first thing you should do is* wash your hands.
Before S + V, S + V.	*Before* you cut up the vegetables, you need to wash them.
After / When S + V, S + V. *After that*, S + V.	*After* you cut up the vegetables, you need to add them to the salad. *After that*, you need to mix the ingredients.
The last / final step is… *Finally*, …	*The last step is* adding your favorite salad dressing. *Finally*, you should add your favorite salad dressing.

Showing Cause and Effect

Words and phrases	Examples
Because S+ V, S + V. S + V *because* S + V. *Because of* NOUN, S + V. S + V *because of* NOUN.	*Because* I broke my leg, I could not move. I could not move *because* I broke my leg. *Because of* my broken leg, I could not move. I could not move *because of* my broken leg.
CAUSE, *so* RESULT.	My sister did not know what to do, *so* she asked my mother for advice.

Describing

Words and phrases	Examples
Prepositions of location: *above, across, around, in, near, under*…	The children raced their bikes *around* the school.
Descriptive adjectives: *wonderful, delightful, dangerous, informative, rusty*…	The *bent, rusty* bike squeaked when I rode it.
SUBJECT + *BE* + ADJECTIVE.	The Terra Cotta Warriors of Xian *are amazing*.
SUBJECT + *BE* + *the most* ADJECTIVE + NOUN.	To me, Thailand *is the most* interesting country in the world.
SUBJECT *tastes / looks / smells / feels like* NOUN.	My ID card *looks like* a credit card.

SUBJECT + BE + *known / famous for its* NOUN.	France *is famous for its* cheese.
Adverbs of manner: *quickly, slowly, quietly, happily…*	I *quickly* wrote his phone number on a scrap of paper that I found on the table.

Stating an Opinion

Words and phrases	Examples
Personally, I believe / think / feel / agree / disagree / suppose (*that*) S + V.	*Personally, I believe that* New York City should ban large sugary drinks.
VERB + *-ING should not be allowed.*	*Smoking* in public *should not be allowed.*
In my opinion / view / experience, S + V.	*In my opinion,* smoking is rude.
For this reason, S + V. *That is why I think that* S + V.	*That is why I think that* smoking should not be allowed in restaurants.
There are many benefits / advantages to VERB + *-ING.*	*There are many benefits to* swimming every day.
There are many drawbacks / disadvantages to VERB + *-ING.*	*There are many drawbacks to* eating most of your meals at a restaurant.
I prefer X [NOUN] *to* Y [NOUN].	*I prefer* soccer *to* football.
To me, VERB + *-ING makes* (*perfect*) *sense.*	*To me,* exercising every day *makes perfect sense.*
For all of these important reasons, I think / believe (*that*) S + V.	*For all of these important reasons, I think* smoking is bad for your health.

Arguing and Persuading

Words and phrases	Examples
It is important to remember that S+V.	*It is important to remember that* students only wear their uniforms during school hours.
According to a recent survey / poll, S + V.	*According to a recent poll,* 85 percent of high school students felt they had too much homework.
Even more important, S + V.	*Even more important,* statistics show the positive effects of school uniforms on student behavior.
SUBJECT *must / should / ought to* VERB.	Researchers *must* stop unethical animal testing.
I agree that S + V. *However,* S + V.	*I agree that* eating healthily is important. *However,* the government should not make food choices for us.

Reacting/Responding

Words and phrases	Examples
TITLE *by* AUTHOR *is a / an* (ADJECTIVE) NOUN.	*Harry Potter and the Goblet of Fire* by J.K. Rowling *is an* entertaining book to read.
My first reaction to the prompt / news / article / question was / is NOUN.	*My first reaction to the article was* anger.
When I read / looked at / thought about NOUN, *I was amazed / shocked / surprised…*	*When I read* the article, *I was surprised* to learn of his athletic ability.

Appendices

Appendix 1

Building Better Sentences

Being a good writer involves many skills including correct grammar usage, varied vocabulary, and conciseness (avoiding unnecessary words). Some student writers like to keep their sentences simple. They feel that they will make mistakes if they write longer, more complicated sentences. However, writing short, choppy sentences one after the other is not considered appropriate in academic writing. Study the examples below.

The time was yesterday.

It was afternoon.

There was a storm.

The storm was strong.

The movement of the storm was quick.

The storm moved towards the coast.

The coast was in North Carolina.

Notice that every sentence has an important piece of information. A good writer would not write all these sentences separately. Instead, the most important information from each sentence can be used to create ONE longer, coherent sentence.

Read the sentences again; this time, the important information has been circled.

The time was (yesterday.)

It was (afternoon.)

There was a (storm.)

The storm was (strong.)

The (movement) of the storm was (quick.)

The storm (moved towards the coast.)

The coast was in (North Carolina.)

Here are some strategies for taking the circled information and creating a new sentence.

1. Create time phrases to begin or end a sentence: yesterday + afternoon

2. Find the key noun: storm

3. Find key adjectives: strong

4. Create noun phrases: a strong + storm

5. Change word forms: movement = move; quick = quickly
   moved + quickly

6. Create place phrases: towards the coast
   towards the coast (of North Carolina)
   or
   towards the North Carolina coast

Better Sentence:

Yesterday afternoon, a strong storm moved quickly towards the North Carolina coast.

Here are some other strategies for building better sentences.

7. Use connectors and transition words.

8. Use pronouns to replace frequently used nouns.

9. Use possessive adjectives and pronouns.

Study the following example:

(Susan) (went) somewhere. That place was (the mall.) Susan wanted to (buy new shoes.)
The shoes were for (Susan's mother.)

Improved, Longer Sentence:

Susan went to the mall because she wanted to buy new shoes for her mother.

Practices

Follow these steps for each practice:

Step 1: Read the sentences. Circle the most important information in each sentence.

Step 2: Write an original sentence from the information you circled. Use the strategies listed on pages 252–253. Remember that there is more than one way to combine sentences.

Practice 1 Unit 1

A. 1. (Tina) is my (friend.)

  2. Tina (works.)

  3. The work is at (Washington Central Bank.)

     My friend Tina works at Washington Central Bank.

  _____

B. 1. There are boxes.

  2. The boxes are on the table.

  3. The boxes are heavy.

     _____

     _____

C. 1. Caroline attends classes.

  2. The classes are at Jefferson Community College.

  3. The classes are on Wednesdays.

     _____

     _____

D. 1. Tuscany is a region.

  2. This region is in Italy.

  3. This region is beautiful.

     _____

     _____

Practice 2 Unit 2

A. 1. There are books.

   2. The books are rare.

   3. The books are in the library.

_____

_____

B. 1. Drivers have more accidents.

   2. The accidents happen on roads.

   3. The roads are snowy.

_____

_____

C. 1. Aspirin is good for headaches.

   2. Aspirin is good for colds.

   3. Aspirin is good for pain.

_____

_____

Practice 3 Unit 3

A. 1. Charlie is a man.

   2. Charlie is my uncle.

   3. Charlie works hard in a restaurant.

   4. The restaurant belongs to Charlie.

_____

_____

B. 1. Tourists often ride boats.

   2. The boats are on the Seine River.

   3. Tourists do this at night.

   4. Tourists do this to see the Eiffel Tower's lights.

   5. The tower's lights are beautiful.

_____

_____

C. 1. Steven is in bed.

    2. It is early.

    3. Steven does this to be ready to work hard.

    4. He is doing this again.

    5. His work is the next day.

_____

_____

Practice 4 Unit 4

A. (Hint: Use a coordinating conjunction.)

    1. Chavez's family received money.

    2. There was very little money.

    3. People treated them badly.

_____

_____

B. (Hint: Use a coordinating conjunction.)

    1. My parents were not rich.

    2. My parents were always happy.

_____

_____

C. 1. This book gives us information.

    2. There is a lot of information.

    3. The book gives us the information now.

    4. The information is important.

    5. The information is about life in the fourteenth century.

_____

_____

Practice 5 Unit 5

A. (Hint: Use a coordinating conjunction.)

    1. Angela needs to buy some fruits.

    2. Angela needs to buy some vegetables.

    3. Angela is shopping at the farmer's market.

_____

_____

B. 1. Visitors are standing in line.

   2. There are many visitors.

   3. The visitors are also waiting to take pictures.

   4. The pictures are of themselves.

   5. There are ruins in the background.

_____

_____

C. (Hint: Use a coordinating conjunction.)

   1. Lisana is working.

   2. This company works with computers.

   3. Lisana does not have a computer engineering degree.

_____

_____

Practice 6 Unit 6

A. (HINT: Create a complex sentence.)

   1. First, Carmen arrives.

   2. Then Carmen will perform some dances.

   3. These dances will be formal.

   4. Carmen will do these dances with her friends.

_____

_____

B. (HINT: Create a complex sentence.)

   1. I go to the theater.

   2. The theater is on Broadway.

   3. I do this often.

   4. The reason I do this is that I live in New York.

_____

_____

C. (HINT: Create a complex sentence.)

1. First, I will arrive in Canada.

2. Next, I am going to buy a lot of souvenirs.

3. There will be souvenirs for my parents.

4. There will be souvenirs for my brother.

5. There will be souvenirs for my friends.

_____

_____

Practice 7 Unit 7

A. (HINT: Use an adjective clause.)

1. The two women are my grandmother and my mother.

2. The women are sitting on the sofa.

_____

_____

B. (HINT: Use an adjective clause.)

1. These are words.

2. There are just a few of these words.

3. These words cause problems for English speakers.

4. These problems are with spelling.

5. These speakers are native and nonnative.

_____

_____

C. 1. Jenna is eating lunch.

2. Jenna is talking to her friends.

3. Jenna is in the cafeteria.

4. Jenna is doing these things right now.

_____

_____

Appendix 2

Extra Writing Activities

WRITING ACTIVITY 1 **Writing a Paragraph (Unit 2)**

Read the paragraph, and follow the steps below to create a new paragraph. Write the new paragraph on the lines provided.

Example Paragraph 75

California

¹California is a large state. ²It is located in the western part of the United States. ³The population of California is approximately 38 million. ⁴The biggest cities in California are Los Angeles and San Francisco. ⁵Millions of tourists visit this state every year. ⁶They come for the beaches, the mountains, and the great weather that this large state is famous for.

1. In Sentences 1, 3, and 4, change *California* to *Florida*. Do the same for the title.

2. In Sentence 2, change *western* to *southeastern*.

3. In Sentence 3, change the population number from *38 million* to *19 million*.

4. In Sentence 4, change the names of the cities from *Los Angeles and San Francisco* to *Miami, Tampa, and Orlando*.

5. In Sentence 6, change *mountains* to *theme parks*.

6. In Sentence 6, change *great weather* to *relaxing life*.

_____

_____

_____

_____

_____

_____

_____

_____

_____

_____

Read the paragraph, and follow the steps below to create a new paragraph. Write the new paragraph on the lines provided.

Example Paragraph 76

My Older Sister

[1]I would like to tell you about my older sister. [2]Her name is Natalie. [3]She is 26 years old. [4]She is an elementary school teacher. [5]She loves children. [6]She is very patient and kind. [7]My sister Natalie is a wonderful person.

1. In Sentences 1 and 7, change *sister* to *brother*. Do the same for the title.
2. In Sentences 3, 4, 5, and 6, change *she* to *he*.
3. In Sentence 2, change *her* to *his*. Be sure to use a capital letter.
4. *Natalie* is a girl's name. In Sentences 2 and 7, change *Natalie* to a boy's name of your choice.
5. In sentence 7, change *wonderful* to *great*.

_____

_____

_____

_____

_____

_____

_____

_____

_____

_____

Read the paragraph, and follow the steps below to create a new paragraph. Write the new paragraph on the lines provided.

Example Paragraph 77

My House

^{1}I live in a big house. ^{2}It is located on Princeton Street. ^{3}My house number is 915. ^{4}My house is new. ^{5}It is two years old. ^{6}The sides of my house are light yellow. ^{7}The roof is light gray. ^{8}In front of the house, there are many flowers. ^{9}I am so lucky to live in this house!

1. In Sentence 1, change *big* to *little*.

2. In Sentence 2, change the name of the street from *Princeton Street* to *Hillside Road.*

3. In Sentence 3, change the house number from *915* to *710.*

4. In Sentence 4, change *new* to *very old.*

5. In Sentence 5, change the number *two* to an appropriate number for a very old house.

6. In Sentences 6 and 7, change the color of the sides of the house from *light yellow* to *white.* Change the color of the roof from *light gray* to *dark gray.*

7. In Sentence 8, change the phrase *many flowers* to *some small bushes and trees.*

8. The current title is simple. Write a better or more interesting title for your paragraph.

_____

_____

_____

_____

_____

_____

_____

_____

_____

_____

Fill in each blank with the correct subject pronoun (*they*, *she*, *he*, or *it*) for the noun(s) in parentheses ( ). Then copy the new paragraph on the lines below. Give the paragraph a title.

Example Paragraph 78

Susan Brown and Joe Chen are actors. (**1.** Susan and Joe)

_____ have very interesting careers. Susan acts in plays in the

theater. (**2.** Susan) _____ works in New York City. (**3.** New York

City) _____ is the best place to work in the theater. Joe acts in

movies. (**4.** Joe) _____ works in Los Angeles. (**5.** Los Angeles)

_____ is an exciting city. (**6.** Film studios) _____ make

lots of movies there. Susan and Joe are very happy with their jobs.

(**7.** Susan and Joe) _____ would not do anything else.

_____

_____

_____

_____

_____

_____

_____

_____

_____

_____

_____

_____

_____

_____

Read the paragraph, and follow the steps below to create a new paragraph. Write the new paragraph on the lines provided.

Example Paragraph 79

A Desert Plant

¹The cactus is an interesting plant. ²It grows in the desert. ³It likes very hot temperatures. ⁴It does not need a lot of water to live. ⁵Its leaves are spiky. ⁶Many people grow this special plant in their gardens.

1. In Sentence 1, change *the cactus* to *seaweed*.
2. In Sentence 2, change *desert* to *ocean*. Do the same in the title, and also change *a* to *an*.
3. In Sentence 3, make the verb *likes* negative.
4. In Sentence 4, make the verb *does not need* affirmative.
5. In Sentence 5, change *spiky* to *long and thin*.
6. In Sentence 6, change *gardens* to *aquariums*.

_____

_____

_____

_____

_____

_____

_____

_____

_____

The paragraph below is missing three sentences. Combine the sentences that follow the paragraph. Use *and*, *but*, or *so*. Then write the three new sentences in the correct place in the paragraph.

Example Paragraph 80

Brandon's New Career

Brandon is studying nursing. **1** _____ _____ _____

Brandon also practices nursing at a local hospital. **2** _____ _____ _____

He is not ready to do that yet. **3** _____ _____

_____ Because of this, it will be easy for him to get a good job. Then he can help as many people as possible.

Missing Sentence 1:   He has to go to school five days a week.
                      He takes several classes every day.

Missing Sentence 2:   He helps with everyday work there.
                      He cannot help with emergencies.

Missing Sentence 3:   Brandon's grades are very good.
                      He will graduate with honors.

Read the paragraph, and follow the steps below to create a new paragraph. Write the new paragraph on the lines provided.

Example Paragraph 81

Life on the Farm

¹My grandpa is a very busy farmer. ²Every day, he gets up at four o'clock in the morning. ³He eats breakfast. ⁴Then he goes out to the barn. ⁵There he feeds and milks the cows. ⁶When he finishes, he feeds the rest of the animals. ⁷Then he works in the cornfields until noon. ⁸He eats a fast lunch. ⁹After that, he works in the fields again. ¹⁰In the evening, he eats dinner. ¹¹Then he feeds the animals one last time. ¹²Grandpa finally goes to bed at around nine o'clock. ¹³He certainly does a lot in one day!

1. In Sentence 2, change *every day* to *yesterday.*

2. In Sentences 2–13, change all the verbs to simple past tense. Be careful of irregular verbs!

Life on the Farm

_____

_____

_____

_____

_____

_____

_____

_____

_____

_____

_____

_____

Read the paragraph, and follow the steps below to create a new paragraph. Write the new paragraph on the lines provided.

Example Paragraph 82

A Memorable Vacation

¹When I was thirteen years old, my aunt and uncle took me on a wonderful vacation. ²We went to the Black Hills in South Dakota. ³We did lots of interesting things. ⁴We visited Mt. Rushmore and took lots of pictures. ⁵We visited a place to mine for gold. ⁶One night, we even ate buffalo burgers for dinner. ⁷It was very exciting. ⁸I made memories on that trip that I will keep for a lifetime.

1. In Sentence 1, change *When I was thirteen years old* to *When I graduate from high school this year*.

2. Change all the verbs in the paragraph to *be going to* + verb.

A Memorable Vacation

_____

_____

_____

_____

_____

_____

_____

_____

_____

_____

_____

_____

_____

Read the paragraph below. Then combine each underlined pair of sentences by using an adjective clause. Rewrite the paragraph with your new sentences on the lines provided.

Example Paragraph 83

The Discovery of the *Titanic*

[1]There were many scientists and explorers. They searched for the *Titanic* for a long time. They finally found it in 1985. It was deep in the Atlantic Ocean. The water was too deep for humans to visit without protection. Scientists solved this problem. [2]In order to explore the wreck, they used a **submersible**. This submersible was **controlled** by people on the surface of the ocean. Explorers took pictures of the *Titanic* with the submersible. [3]They even brought things to the surface. These things were on the **sunken** ship. Because of these people's efforts, we now understand more about the remains of the *Titanic*.

a submersible: a vehicle that can go very deep underwater

to control: to guide

sunken: covered by water

The Discovery of the *Titanic*

There were many scientists and explorers who searched for the <u>Titanic</u> for a long time.

_____

_____

_____

_____

_____

_____

_____

_____

_____

_____

_____

_____

_____

Appendix 3

Peer Editing Sheet Sample

This is an example of the Peer Editing Sheets available for *Great Writing 1: Great Sentences for Great Paragraphs.* To print them out, go to NGL.Cengage.com/GW1.

Unit 1

Writer: _____ Date: _____

Peer Editor: _____

1. What country did the writer write about? _____

2. How many sentences did the writer write? _____

3. Does each sentence begin with a capital letter?   ❏ yes   ❏ no

   If not, which sentences need to be fixed?

   _____

   _____

   _____

   _____

4. Does each sentence have a period, question mark, or exclamation point at the end?   ❏ yes   ❏ no

   If not, which sentences need to be fixed? _____

   _____

   _____

5. What is the longest sentence? _____

   _____

   How many words does it have? _____

6. Do you see an error in any of the sentences?   ❏ yes   ❏ no

   If so, write one of the sentences here, but correct the error.

   _____

   _____

Index